"In *Agnostic at the Altar*, Dr. John Van Hagen offers a remarkably thoughtful, scholarly, yet highly personal reflection on the stories and wisdom of the great Jewish prophets such as Elijah, Ezekiel, Amos, Jeremiah, and Jesus in an attempt to better understand and appreciate the spiritual and transcendent nature of the Judeo-Christian tradition through these prophetic models. Dr. Van Hagen, like so many people today, is agnostic yet searching for meaning, purpose, wisdom, and truth through the stories told within the Judeo-Christian worldview. Anyone interested in a deeper appreciation and better understanding of these spiritual and religious giants within these faith traditions will absolutely love this book and won't be able to put it down."

—THOMAS PLANTE
Santa Clara University

"In *Agnostic at the Altar*, John Van Hagen, a clinical psychologist and former priest, takes us on a scholarly, but also very personal journey as he searches for transcendence in the writings of the Old Testament prophets. Most agnostics have separated themselves from institutional religion, but Van Hagen, in his reflective agnosticism, is delving into the heart of religion in the stories of the Jewish prophets in order to find a middle ground between the deficits of organized religion and his need for transcendence. For anyone today who struggles with the failures of organized religion, who wonders where God is amidst the chaos, destruction, and anguish in the world, and yet who still is drawn to the transcendent, *Agnostic at the Altar* is a timely, well written, comforting, and valuable resource."

—BRIAN CAHILL
author of *Cops, Cons and Grace*

"Van Hagen combines an honest agnosticism with critical biblical scholarship, his insights as a psychologist, and an open-eyed awareness of both the blessings and toxins of organized religion to share what we can learn from the Jewish prophets (including Jesus) about embracing the ambiguities of our time as we strive for moral clarity and religious integrity."

—Robert Miller
Juniata College

"John Van Hagen has written a book that is about his struggles with the stories of the prophets while contemplating his place at the altar of his church. Yet it reminded me of Jacob's wrestling with an angel. In this book, Dr. Van Hagen wrestles with destroying angels, the angels of our better natures and the angels of ancient times and legend. He wrestles with the prophets of the Bible, engaging them to wrest from them their historical context, their personalities, their unique visions and lessons of wisdom, social justice and the meaning of a life of value. His gifts as both psychologist and priest give the reader victory over ignorance, blind faith, and meaninglessness. A historical, contextual, well reasoned critical engagement that offers much."

—David Greenwald
author

Agnostic at the Altar

Agnostic at the Altar

Searching for Transcendence
in the Story of the Prophets

JOHN VAN HAGEN

Foreword by Thomas Sheehan

WIPF & STOCK · Eugene, Oregon

AGNOSTIC AT THE ALTAR
Searching for Transcendence in the Story of the Prophets

Copyright © 2019 John Van Hagen. All rights reserved. Except for brief quotations in critical publications or reviews, no part of this book may be reproduced in any manner without prior written permission from the publisher. Write: Permissions, Wipf and Stock Publishers, 199 W. 8th Ave., Suite 3, Eugene, OR 97401.

Wipf & Stock
An Imprint of Wipf and Stock Publishers
199 W. 8th Ave., Suite 3
Eugene, OR 97401

www.wipfandstock.com

PAPERBACK ISBN: 978-1-5326-7580-5
HARDCOVER ISBN: 978-1-5326-7581-2
EBOOK ISBN: 978-1-5326-7582-9

Manufactured in the U.S.A.   APRIL 22, 2019

Scripture quotations contained herein are from the New Revised Standard Version Bible © 1989 by the division of Christian Education of the National Council of the Churches of Christ in the U.S.A. Used by permission. All rights reserved.

Illustrated map of Samaria and Judah taken from Wikipedia. Used by permission. All rights reserved.

Illustrated map of Assyrian Empire taken from Wikipedia. Used by permission. All rights reserved.

Illustrated map of the Pilgrim Route to Jerusalem taken from *Luke* by Robert Vinson, Smyth & Helwys Publishing (2008). Used by permission. Some of the material in chapters 4, 6, and 7 was previously published in Westar's *The Fourth R*.

Dedicated to our grandchildren Atticus, Elouise, and Lena: May the gift of wonder, given to you by your wonderful parents, stay with you throughout your lives.

But once kindled, the spark of transcendence is never fully lost. It remains buried within the tradition as a heritage of hope.

RICHARD MADSEN

Contents

Illustrations | ix
Foreword by Thomas Sheehan | xi
Preface | xvii
Introduction | xxi

1. The Jewish Prophets in Context | 1
2. Elijah: The Once and Future Prophet | 9
3. Amos: The Prophet of Justice | 22
4. Ezekiel: A Cautionary Tale | 33
5. The Prophet Jeremiah as Existential Hero? | 42
6. Isaiah: Three Prophets in One Book | 52
7. The Changing Story of Jesus, the Prophet | 69
8. Science: A New Context for the Prophets' Story? | 84

Conclusion | 97

Bibliography | 105
Index | 109

List of Illustrations

Map of Samaria and Judah | 10

Map of the Assyrian Empire that surrounded Judah | 12

Map of the route that religious pilgrims took
to travel south to Jerusalem | 75

Foreword

WITH THIS, HIS SECOND book, John Van Hagen continues to disprove F. Scott Fitzgerald's claim that there are no second acts in American lives. In fact, there may even be third acts.
John Van Hagen began his career as a Roman Catholic priest in San Francisco. After serving in ministry for two-and-a-half years, he resigned, married, and went on to earn a PhD in psychology at Adelphi University. Now in retirement after over thirty years as a therapist, Van Hagen has been focusing his considerable talents on important, if controversial, questions in religion and biblical scholarship.

His highly successful *Rescuing Religion: How Faith Can Survive Its Encounter with Science* (2012) confronted the crisis of cognitive dissonance within Christianity that has been brought on by advances in archeology, biblical studies, and historical science. Now, with *Agnostic at the Altar*, he tackles the complex issue of the Hebrew prophets and, more broadly, the role that stories—both religious and secular—can play in forging meaning in moments of existential crisis. Those familiar with his first book will find in the present volume the same critical but constructive effort at conjugating science and spirituality to create a viable path into our post-modern future.

In the spirit of Karl Jaspers, Shmuel Eisenstadt, and Robert Bellah, Van Hagen anchors this treatise in what has come to be called the Axial Age (ca. 700 to 200 BCE). Those centuries saw a revolutionary new self-understanding break through decaying

Foreword

ideologies and exhibit notable commonalities across cultural forms as diverse as Confucianism in China, Buddhism in India, Zoroastrianism in Persia, philosophy in Greece, and ethical prophecy in Israel.

With the collapse of the Bronze Age, the emerging Iron Age witnessed radical changes in the economic, socio-political, and religious configuration of the Near East. Those changes included the invention of the abacus, the first known use of coinage, and a critical revolution in writing. While cuneiform and hieroglyphic scripts date back to the mid-fourth millennium, the late Bronze Age invention of alphabets liberated writing from the delimited circles of court scribes and accountants and spread literacy to a wider demographic, including itinerant prophets like Amos, Hosea, and their disciples in the mid-eighth century Palestine.

The Axial Age saw a momentous religious shift away from the archaic cosmo-political ideology in which the king was the representative of the local high god, and sometimes even the god's avatar. The emergence of a new reflexivity—a thinking *about* one's thinking—inspired a radical questioning of received traditions and led to new *universalist* understandings of reality, including alternative models of the relation of the divine and the human. Enter the phenomenon of the Hebrew prophets who flourished from roughly 850 to 550 BCE, with their unique emphasis on ethical monotheism.

The Israelites did not invent prophecy as such. The Hebrew word nābî' (plural nebî'îm) likely derives from an ancient Akkadian term for "one who is sent to speak." With the Septuagint, the translation of the Hebrew Bible into Greek beginning in the third century BCE, the word nābî' was translated as προφήτης (prophētēs), "prophet" in the sense of someone who speaks

1. in public,
2. on behalf of Yahweh,
3. with regard to urgent present issues.

Foreword

The prophet's words were directed to *present* crises, whereas the notion of prophecy as predicting the *future* derives from the later apocalyptic literature, for example, the book of Daniel in the Hebrew Bible and the book of Revelation in the New Testament. To be sure, the Hebrew prophets often warned of imminent disaster and sometimes imagined a utopian future, but the future, whether dystopic or utopic, was always linked to the present conduct of the prophet's audience: immoral and unfaithful in the one case, ethical and faithful in the other.

Van Hagen focuses on "classical" prophecy, that is, not the pre-monarchical nebî'îm who proclaimed patriotic oracles against the Philistines during the period of the judges, ca. 1200–1000 (see 1 Sam 10), nor the prophets like Nathan (2 Sam 7 and 12) who worked for the royal court during the Davidic monarchy between ca.1010 and 970 BCE. Instead, Van Hagen deals with the prophets who labored first in the divided kingdoms that followed the death of Solomon (931 BCE) and then during and after the Babylonian Exile (587–538 BCE), that is, in

1. the Northern Kingdom of Israel, in Samaria (ca. 930–720)
   - Elijah (ca. 870–850 BCE)
   - Amos (ca. 750 BCE)

2. the Southern Kingdom of Judah, centered in Jerusalem (ca. 1030–587 BCE)
   - First (or Proto-) Isaiah (ca. 740–700 BCE)
   - Jeremiah (ca. 625–587 BCE)
   - Ezekiel (? ca. 587 BCE; scholars debate whether his ministry was in Palestine, Babylon, or both)

3. the Babylonian Exile (ca. 587–538 BCE)
   - Ezekiel (? after 587 BCE: see immediately above)
   - Second (or Deutero-) Isaiah (ca. 540 BCE)

4. the immediate post-exilic period (ca. 538–515 BCE; in Palestine, under Persian rule)
   - Third (or Trito-) Isaiah

What Van Hagen finds coursing through all these diverse voices—whether in Elijah's (often violent) cathexis on Yahweh, Amos' call for justice, Ezekiel's hope that God will give his people a new heart, or Jeremiah's existential suffering—is a search for a radical *transcendence* that would bind the Israelites to a *universal* God who would forge a *new identity* for his people. If there is one figure among these prophets who most exemplifies this Axial Age revolution, it would be Second Isaiah, who breaks through the confines of residual tribism and proclaims a theology of world history centered on an utterly transcendent Yahweh who offers salvation to all nations.

Van Hagen takes one further step, and a very controversial one, by interpreting Yeshua of Nazareth as a latter-day prophet in the mold of Elijah and Amos. Van Hagen calls for a "minimalist" view of Yeshua/Jesus, neither as the long-awaited Messiah of the Synoptic Gospels nor as the divine Son of God of Johannine theology, but rather as an itinerant preacher of justice and mercy among the poor of Galilee, who were oppressed from without by Roman imperialism and crushed from within by the country's ruthless economy. As for what transpired after the death of Jesus, Van Hagen underlines the would-be universalism of Pauline theology and the gentile-friendliness of Luke's Gospel. However, in the supercessionism of the Christian apologist Justin (fl. ca. 130–160 CE)—for all its efforts to universalize Jesus into the Logos of the entire cosmos—he finds the seeds of two millennia of anti-Jewish violence and murder.

But what about Van Hagen the agnostic? And with reference to the title this volume, what altar is he standing at, and what kind of transcendence does he think possible?

His book is both fully informed by contemporary biblical scholarship and sensitively attuned of the post-religious culture of the present day, and thus his reading of the prophets is both deeply appreciative and acutely critical. Their efforts to craft a story of community, hope, and social survival is one that he seeks to retrieve and refashion for today—but without its religious pathologies, its fixation on an all-powerful and often violent deity who dispenses rewards or punishments depending on the obedience or not of his subjects, not to mention the authoritarianism exercised by his religious representatives on earth. Van Hagen characterizes the God of the prophets *and* of Christianity as "a character in someone else's story"—in fact, a character in a *fiction* that both Hebrew prophets and Christian theologians have tried to pass off as *history*.

In the shadow of this book lies Nietzsche's proclamation of the death of God: the final demise of a supernaturally transcendent realm, and the bending of the axis of transcendence from the vertical to the horizontal, from eternity to history, from a timeless and ever-stable Beyond to an open-ended and very uncertain future. Van Hagen finds the locus of personal and social meaning to reside in communally shared stories: no story, no meaning. In stories, as in life, context is all, and context is social, dynamic, and open-ended. Stories are about a "whole," not a complete and self-enclosed totality that encompasses everything, but an ever-changing and relatively coherent network of references and referrals—among persons, things, events, whatever—that lets us make tentative sense of a past whose origin we cannot see, a present whose depths we cannot fathom, and a future whose final outcome we will never see. "*Homo abyssus est*," St. Augustine wrote: human being is a bottomless abyss. And whereas Augustine and other believers may hold that God encompasses that abyss and holds everyone in loving security, the agnostic has no experience of that, whether by faith, reason, hope, or intimation. And yet even the agnostic needs a story.

Nietzsche labeled Christianity as nothing more than "Platonism for the masses," and his proclamation of the death of God was really an obituary for all such Platonisms. Van Hagen makes his own Nietzsche's claim that in our own day the so-called "true world"—the supernatural Beyond of religions, the Absolute Truth of traditional philosophy—has been proven itself a fable. Nietzsche's hope was that, with the demise of that fable, "all who are born after us will be part of a higher history than all history up to now."

With this book the author invites us to exchange that fable—or whatever Big Story with its Deep Backup and Happy Ending that we may wrap ourselves in—for the *biggest* of big stories, the "Universe Story" of contemporary cosmology: evolution as the scientifically explainable (yet ultimately unfathomable) history of some fourteen billion years thus far and unknowable billions yet to come. Van Hagen reads the Universe Story, at least in its present moment, as a *human* story, not least of all because it is we who tell that story (we are evolution become conscious of itself) and because it is we who are *living* that story. With such telling and living there comes the call to *make* that story our own. It is ours to become, and the call is to actually make it a *human* story—that is, a moral story—in the best and most inclusive way.

The prophet Amos's millennia-old call for justice, above and beyond all forms of religion, resonates emphatically in the powerful final chapters of this book. The challenge that echoes from that call concerns the "how" of such an immense task: how to live together and carry forward as a community the economic, social, and political struggles that might justify Nietzsche's hope of a "higher history" for those who come after us.

Evolution is the reality of the universe and of ourselves: a constant, on-going emergence of energy become matter become human become (we may hope) *truly* human: transcendent towards a universality in which no one is really free until all are free. The call is to become as radical as reality itself.

Thomas Sheehan
Stanford University

Preface

I WAS DISCUSSING THE lack of overtly religious interest in the lives of our adult children with a retired bishop who has written extensively on the church's need for reform. At one point he looked off into the distance and complained, "The church has lost the youth, the church has lost the intellectuals, and if it doesn't change . . ." He never completed the sentence, but I think I knew what he meant: the church will continue to lose whole groups of people if it fails to reform itself.

I share that bishop's bleak prediction, but for different reasons. In order to reform itself, the church would have to give up the markers that identified it as something special and unique: extensive beliefs in a supernatural world, a corresponding version of history, and a parochial code of ethics. More important, it would need to give up the claim that such identity markers were divinely given and therefore irrevocable. However, whether or not we are members of a religious organization, we can develop a religious orientation that can take us where that church or religious group cannot go. The starting point is not the received tradition, but rather the individual experience that reveals that there is something beyond ourselves.

I have written this book for anyone who remembers a sudden insight or intuition that led to a deeper meaning and wants to keep alive that experience of the transcendent. My own experience was heavily clothed in religious and spiritual stories. But it doesn't have to be. It could simply be a glimpse into a deeper appreciation of

Preface

life and, implicitly, a connection to all who share in that life. The experience could have happened at a time of crisis or at the end of the more methodical search for understanding. It could even have been associated with an appreciation that spirituality is part of our makeup, and to deny its existence is to cut ourselves off from something that enriches our lives.

The spiritual experience also has a heroic dimension. It can motivate a person to follow a path to an uncertain future, despite the difficulties in such an undertaking. Even if the journey is quiet and the accomplishments modest, the effort gives a glimpse into what motivated heroic men and women to work for something much larger than themselves, and, in doing so, to help others. Our heroes are usually drawn from our culture and times, but a cluster of them can be found in a period of history called the Axial Age, a brief period centered around the sixth century BCE and containing such prophetic figures as Confucius and the Buddha.

This book focuses on some misunderstood Axial Age heroes who lived in a small corner of the ancient world in what came to be known as Palestine: the Jewish prophets. They are often depicted as eccentric loners, who today might be wandering around with sandwich boards that announce the coming end of the world. However, their religious experiences were so profound that they left their mark on Western civilization and helped their own people survive when other peoples did not.

As an agnostic who doubts whether the being described by the prophets truly exists, I still value their insistence that we embrace the power of something larger than ourselves. At one level, living a more spiritual life does wonders for us as we plod along in this mundane one. Yet it is more than self-enhancement. The Jewish prophets are representatives of a global, international insistence that our survival as a species depends on our being open to a transcendent vision that offers a way to peace for our world. If we do not embrace their vision of old and act on it, today's scientists predict we will face something like the calamitous ending the prophets predicted.

Preface

I wrote this book out of a sense of gratitude for the spiritual experiences that enlivened my life and led me to a place I never would have predicted for myself. I also wrote it as an insurance policy to help me keep those experiences alive by studying their various iterations and remaining open to their unpredictable appearances. The book represents my lifeline to a spiritual world that only can be described inadequately.

I am grateful also to the many well-grounded individuals who have supported my efforts. I especially want to thank my high school English teacher, Fr. Gene Strain, who long ago encouraged me to write; to Tom Sheehan, in whose long-time and caring relationship I learned to think; to Jim and Bernie Purcell and Rich and Ann Laveroni, who have supported my journey in our forty-year-old intentional community by sharing their own stories.

I am thankful to the ongoing educational work of Westar, especially to Bob Miller, who over the years has edited my early attempts at articulating my ideas in Westar's journal, *The Fourth R*. I am also grateful for the support of Matthew Wimer and the staff at Wipf and Stock who, together with Julie McCarron, offered the creative and technical assistance that transformed a manuscript into a book. And, most of all, thank you, Phyllis. You are my loving lifeline to this world even as I sail off to explore that other one.

Introduction

The desire to cultivate a sense of the transcendent may be *the* defining human characteristic.

KAREN ARMSTRONG, *THE CASE FOR GOD*

Agnostic at the Altar?

RELIGION IS A SEARCH for transcendence: that sense of something beyond or far greater than ourselves. While people the world over are increasingly aware that religious practices and a spiritual orientation add to our quality of life, at the same time they question the dogmatic explanations of religion or science.[1] The growing number of those professing no religious affiliation (the "nones") exemplify a trend toward an increasing abandonment of traditional forms of religion. Spirituality—the search for meaning in life—continues to become evermore self-oriented and idiosyncratic.

Agnosticism—the belief that the existence of a higher power such as God cannot be proven or disproven—speaks to the gap between our experience of a force larger than ourselves, like love or justice, and our awkward attempts to put words around that experience. Is there truly a God who embodies these transcendental qualities and communicates them to us in some mysterious fashion? Or do these experiences arise from our own consciousness as we instinctively seek to grasp what is good for us and for others?

1. Nagel, *Mind and Cosmos*, 4–12.

Introduction

    Many who tell the story of the universe are influenced by their own religious background and color scientific data with their personal sense of the transcendent. An agnostic takes the opposite approach and uses scientific methodology and critical thinking to understand and appreciate the importance of the transcendent in human evolution, without positing a belief in God. This position is similar to scientists who marvel at the process of self-regulation and the emergence of interdependent life in our universe. They, too, feel a sense of awe, ineffable wonder, and gratitude in the presence of such mysteries, while not necessarily subscribing to a particular religious point of view.

    The brief experience of the transcendent can motivate an agnostic to approach the altar—in my case, a Christian church. My own spiritual journey began when I was in the sixth grade at my local Catholic elementary school. The nuns there had encouraged us to "visit Jesus" during the forty hours of devotion that weekend. When I arrived, the only other occupants of the church were two of the sisters, who had apparently been there for some time. They almost immediately approached the pew where I was kneeling, and one of them kindly but firmly suggested I stay with Jesus until someone else arrived. "We don't want to let Jesus be lonely," she said, and then they left me alone. I was soon engaged in a fairly relaxed but more or less one-way conversation with the now very human and vulnerable Jesus. In this brief encounter I had a sense of being called to service.

    Although I could not articulate it at the time, this experience opened up another dimension for me. For a moment, the everyday world I found so confusing—if not downright strange—disappeared, and a new one opened up in which there was order, direction, and meaning. I was determined to become a citizen of this alternative world in which Jesus guided us to help those less fortunate ones trapped in an everyday existence surrounded by confusion and meaninglessness. I had been secretly called to help them, and I would remain at the ready until I was summoned to begin my mission.

    My mission began with entering a Catholic seminary at age fourteen and being ordained as a priest at twenty-six, then leaving

Introduction

ministry, marrying, and becoming a psychologist a few years later. Although I have continued to attend church, my own life experiences and exploration of Christianity's history and truth claims eventually led me to see that God was a character in someone else's story. Abandoning that story to construct my own left me with a dilemma: Where do I start?

Total rejection of religion meant that I would have no venue to celebrate the experiences of the transcendent that had so dramatically influenced my life's course. And the quest was not just about me. In an earlier book, I argued that a scientific explanation of religion had yet to explain the therapeutic power of spiritual values upon our lives,[2] even though people who have experienced a transforming spiritual power tend to demonstrate better adjustment and psychological health.[3] I chose to continue attending church because my life had been guided by something transcendent. I chose to be grateful for those experiences, but stay agnostic about their ultimate meaning.

Armed with information and insights that protected me from the church's more noxious elements, I created a safe place where I could engage with that transcendent force that I found so empowering. While being receptive to what others call a higher power, I now scrutinize the church's rituals and stories as a way to create some distance from the underlying message: humanity's abject sinfulness while prizing obedience and loyalty to its storytellers. Thus protected, I listen for those traces of the transcendent I often unexpectedly experience.

I found the stories of the prophets especially engaging. Their stories tell of passionate individuals who were driven by a mighty force they called Yahweh to speak and act with remarkable courage and self-sacrifice. That force was so real to them that one can still feel it after all these centuries. Their call to action was often dramatic, but it could also be experienced as a quiet, prayer-like voice. That latter description particularly resonated because it is common to my own: the gentle voice offering insight into what

---

2. Van Hagen, *Rescuing Religion*, 218–20.
3. Hamer, *God Gene*, 5–6.

Introduction

is real. Even so, these stories also described a transcendent power that at times demanded unthinking obedience and a heartless attitude toward those who believe in different stories.

The Jewish prophets told stories, but over time the stories told them. Originally meant to give hope to a fragile and defeated people, these narratives differed slightly in tone and content, but all had the same three-part arc. They told of a prehistoric Golden Age when the people enjoyed a special intimacy with their god; a betrayal of that relationship that demanded they be punished; and, finally, their god's future intervention to establish a utopia on earth that was beyond mankind's ability alone to achieve. In their intimate encounters with their god Yahweh, the prophets experienced a transcendent view of reality and predicted the course of history.

Over time, the lives of the storytellers were embellished. Eventually the prophets became more like superhuman characters whose dramatic roles as speakers for their god became proof of the stories they told. Their status and legends were so persuasive that when the early Christians told their own narrative, they had to reinterpret the prophets to justify the radically new identity they gave to Jesus.

To approach the altar as an agnostic involves a critical sifting through of the particular and parochial in the hope of experiencing a brief taste of what the Jewish prophets experienced, which led them to emphasize justice and right worship as a way toward a just and peaceful future. Comfortable with not knowing whether the God of the prophets exists, an agnostic can still appreciate ritual and community as opportunities to witness and even experience a power greater than oneself. Sharing the ignorance of the prophets about an afterlife, an agnostic focuses on improving this one.

Because descriptions of the transcendent are based on one's personal experience, an agnostic appreciates that such descriptions are often wrong. The challenge is to hold on to the value of the experience while appreciating that there is no protection against error or self-righteousness. Still, there is the commitment to tolerate ambiguity while continuing a never-ending search.

While this book may center upon the intangibles of the philosophical and spiritual dimensions, it also offers a factual context to these Hebrew prophets residing centuries ago in the small neighboring kingdoms of Samaria and Judah. This more factual focus severs the prophets from their long-standing role as predictors of the future or oracles about the coming of Jesus; instead, it permits them to be embedded back into the life-and-death struggles of the Jewish people during the early centuries of their existence in what is now Palestine and Israel. In this age of increasing global tension and strife, I propose that the ancient descriptions for a just way of living together are not just historically interesting, but also in perfect keeping with an evolutionary-based desire that all people live in harmony.

Agnostic at the Altar approaches the traditional with a sense of humility that all stories (including our own) are flawed and with a sense of awe for the work of past spiritual thinkers who dared dream of a better world. Recently, scientists and theologians have projected a spiritual dimension into the new narrative of the universe's journey with its unpredictable evolution from chaos into order, which ultimately produced the life-giving planet Earth. This universal story also speaks of a powerful but mysterious force that self-regulates in order to produce emergent interdependent life forms and ultimately, even consciousness itself.

Whether one engages in the prophets' story, its revised Christian version or the data-driven scientific narrative, one common outcome is to embrace the human struggle between individual flourishing and the more universal concern for others. Being an agnostic can help in the struggle because this position begins with the realization that we are all part of something we will never understand. To be an agnostic allows one to learn from all these of various narratives the value of ambiguity and doubt that is inherent in all the efforts to translate the transcendent into words and actions. It is in the stories of the prophets that I find insights into a spiritual dimension of reality that offers meaning and purpose. Hopefully, this tribute to their courage and genius will do the same for present-day readers.

I

The Jewish Prophets in Context

Yet, in fact, we have never surpassed the insights of the Axial Age.

KAREN ARMSTRONG, *THE GREAT TRANSFORMATION*

THE BRILLIANT EVOLUTIONARY BIOLOGIST Stephen J. Gould concluded in a scientific breakthrough that evolution was not a neat progressive movement but rather an unpredictable record of fits and starts. He held that there were sudden bursts in evolutionary history as new forms dramatically sprang up over relatively brief periods of time. One such time was the Cambrian period, in which many forms of plant and animal life, some previously unknown, emerged on the scene.

Something similar occurred in humankind's spiritual evolution. The sixth century BCE witnessed a unique burst of spiritual activity. As noted by sociologist Rodney Stark, "stretching from China to Israel, many great religious founders were contemporaries: Buddha, Confucius, Lao-Tzu (Taoism), Mahavira (Jainism), the principal authors of the Hindu Upanisads, Zoroaster, even the Israelite prophets Jeremiah and Ezekiel, as well as the biblical author referred to as Second Isaiah, all lived in the sixth century BC."¹ Many other authors have noted this extraordinary phenomenon, usually adding a few centuries before and after the sixth to include important antecedents or significant followers.

Karl Jaspers called this period of time the Axial Age—*axial* because it was a turning point. Humans throughout the known world became more conscious of their limitations, but still strove for "liberation and redemption."² The whole of humanity took a forward leap into a new spiritual world. "The step toward universality was taken in every sense."³ Stark adds that these religious innovators were also concerned about morality, the right way to live in a more complex world.

This book focuses on the Jewish prophets—in particular, the stories they developed about morality, religion, and their own identity as a people. However, they will also be considered in the context of other Axial Age religious innovators who emerged during this evolutionary period. Indeed, to place the Jewish prophets in this moment of evolutionary growth is to stress their universality. Or to put it another way, *all* the spiritual leaders of the Axial Age were prophets.

As scholar Richard Madsen puts it, "They proclaimed that there was a great universal fountain of Truth that existed beyond all of the particular alliances of this world. The search for this Truth and obedience to its demands was the lever for criticism of exclusive myths and particular communities. But the prophets who initiated the Axial traditions were all, in their own ways, against idolatry—the notion that the ultimate Truth could be definitively captured by symbols or institutions constructed by humans."⁴

Prophets of the Axial Age

The life of Confucius (551–479 BCE) is difficult to reconstruct because of the many legends created around him and the attribution

1. Stark, *Why God?*, 58.
2. Jaspers, *Origin*, 2.
3. Jaspers, *Origin*, 2.
4. Madsen, "Future of Transcendence," 441–42.

The Jewish Prophets in Context

of later works to him. According to sociologist Robert Bellah, Confucius was a teacher of the arts who was deeply concerned with the spiritual growth of his students, including their ethical development and moral stance toward the world. Although an innovator, he looked to the past as a time of integrity, which he felt in some way needed to be imitated. "What is clear is that Confucius was a man of extraordinary integrity who made an impression on his students that later generations never forgot."[5]

Roughly contemporary with Confucius of China was the Buddha of India. It is said that the Buddha broke away from his comfortable lifestyle, which included a wife and child, and pursued the life of an ascetic. He developed a rich interior life, which aimed to master suffering, and then passed on his teachings to disciples. Although a monk and seemingly apolitical, the Buddha articulated a number of ethical principles, which he directed his disciples to both model in their lives and to encourage others to follow. These teachings included overcoming the individual yearnings that lead to suffering and a universal message that embraces peace and justice in society. Today, a modern follower of Buddha, the Nobel Peace Prize winner the Dalai Lama, carries on this mission for universal justice.

Likewise, Socrates of Athens (who died in 399 BCE) urged others to examine carefully their own lives and search for truth. Karen Armstrong sees something of Buddha's serenity in the face of suffering in Socrates, "who had discovered something similar to his lifelong discipline of passionate honesty which made him capable of equanimity while undergoing an unjust execution."[6] Building on earlier traditions, the fifth-century Socrates, his student Plato, and other Greek philosophers such as Aristotle worked to provide the ethics arrived at through reason, which could inform a more just society.

It is in this context of Chinese, Indian, and Greek prophets that the Jewish ones should be embedded, because they all described radically new insights that emerged independently in a relatively brief moment of human history. Their commonality

5. Bellah, *Religion in Human Evolution*, 411.
6. Armstrong, *Transformations*, 281.

provided an axis on which human consciousness turned toward a deeper spiritual understanding of human existence. Although each visionary independently offered unique insights into the human condition, together they provided a common message of hope that human beings are able to transcend the circumstances of their lives in order to work for a better society. In addition to this common optimism, they reached similar conclusions about the religious dimension of life they had discovered.

Common Characteristics of the Axial Age Prophets

Otherworldly

What Jaspers sees in these remarkable individuals is a kind of faith, often coming from extended personal struggle. These visionaries imagined a way of being that was in harmony with some higher power. The philosopher Charles Taylor sees the most innovative contribution of the Axial Age as their belief that the cosmos to which we all belong is essentially good. Gone are the gods fighting with each other or a sense of evil pervading the world. Instead, there is the prospect of progress and perfectibility. All may not attain the level of Plato's ideal philosopher or the Buddha's fully awakened disciple, but the possibility for enlightened living was there in our common human nature.[7] Their beliefs marked a break from the traditional religious views that had informed their societies.

    The Buddha broke with his culture by arguing that human flourishing came from renouncing desires through rigorous spiritual practice. The Buddha "was teaching men and women how to transcend the world and its suffering, how to reach beyond human pettiness and expediency and discover an absolute value."[8] Inspired by his legendary "great awakening," Buddha would proclaim knowledge that offered a way to transcend suffering and how to practice the ethical guidelines that led to a meaningful life.

---

7. Taylor, "What Was Axial Revolution?," 30–46.
8. Armstrong, *Buddha*, xxiii.

The Jewish Prophets in Context

For these seekers of the Axial Age, an individual's experience of the transcendent was intimately connected to a call to action. The visions experienced by the Jewish prophets directed them to align themselves with the rule of justice that held sway in Yahweh's heavenly kingdom so they could preach for its echo here on earth. For Confucius, this kind of alignment became visible in behavior through right action, as "the hidden reality of heaven communicates itself to the man who is in harmony with it by his actions."[9]

This-worldly

The insights of these spiritual seekers had implications not only for individuals, but also for society at large; they saw their societies as also out of alignment. The Jewish prophets would rail against the injustice they saw in the economic policies of a developing nation that marginalized the poor and corrupted the judicial system. The more cerebral Plato argued that philosophers should be rulers because only they had developed the kind of integrity that just rulers should possess. Both Confucius and the Buddha exhorted their disciples to relieve the distress and suffering of others in society and in the world.

This exhortation to repair society's ills meant that these religious innovators did not limit their teaching to individual development or personal enlightenment alone; it was meant as a revelation to the world as they saw it. The challenge was to transform society to reflect the good cosmos that everybody belonged to so that it, too, could flourish. "Like the Buddha, Plato insisted that after achieving enlightenment, the sage must return to the 'agora' [public space] and work there for the betterment of humanity."[10]

Evolutionary Progress

Belief in a good cosmos and in the goodness of human nature meant that the spiritual innovators also believed in progress.

9. Merton, *Mystics*, 59.
10. Armstrong, *Transformations*, 314.

Jaspers incorporates this point in the title of his book *The Origin and Goal of History*. Despite living through the destruction of World War II, he hopes for a rebirth: a movement toward a goal to which we are all called to work. In his mind, spiritual evolution is always possible because the Axial Age contributions are our spiritual inheritance, even if their accessibility is sometimes quite difficult.

In fact, many of those that Jaspers identified as spiritual innovators also had to face the terror of war and its aftermath. When their beloved Jerusalem was destroyed and their land devastated by armed conquerors, the Jewish prophets believed that Yahweh would intervene and a New Jerusalem would arise. Confucius lived in a time when the push for unrestrained wealth led to ever-increasing warfare. He believed that an alternative reality was possible—one free of the unbridled use of military power.

Axial Age inventors believed that progress was possible because the world was good, although it might be difficult to see that goodness at times. What was required was the discipline to look within. Also required was the hard work of distancing oneself from a culture that often valorized power and marginalized the poor. To be a disciple of the Buddha meant one first needed to renounce what the prevailing culture saw as important. It was only after this difficult initial step that one could discover the guiding spiritual capacity within oneself.

Progress was possible because we are rational creatures. We observe our behavior and note what was harmful and what was helpful. We examine arguments to find what made sense and what did not. We can see the path that leads to destruction and the one that lead to salvation. The good cosmos meant that we, too, were good, even if it was a struggle to be so.

Engaging the Axial Age Prophets

We view the accomplishments of these very different religious heroes with awe, because they almost simultaneously nudged us to look beyond our world in order to better it. From an evolutionary

The Jewish Prophets in Context

perspective, we can consider them innovative pioneers whose efforts moved our human race into a different level of consciousness. Their combined contributions stand as a reminder that a more just and humane civilization is possible.

However, they lose some of their luster when their legacy is looked at over subsequent centuries. The innovative spiritual heroes of the Axial Age had followers who, over the years, embellished their lives and teachings, making it impossible, for example, to reconstruct accurately the historical Confucius or Buddha. Socrates wrote nothing down; his life and work were assembled by his student, Plato. The original writings of the Jewish prophets were modified over time, adapting them to changing circumstances by disciples trying to make them more relevant in the belief that their insights had everlasting value. Despite their good intentions, disciples would argue with each other and split off into factions, and the search for truth would evolve into deadly competition as to which group best represented that truth.

Placing the Jewish prophets in the turbulent and creative Axial Age means that while their stories may not have been believable, they were on to something. They cannot provide us a blueprint for living in today's world, but they can remind us that the spiritual dimension is part of our heritage as human beings. Although expressing that dimension will always be limited, we can embrace the search for it to learn who we really are and what we are called to do in this world.

The Jewish prophets also struggled with the conflict between the pull to transcendence and the need to survive as a people. How could they promote a universal message of hope to all when their very existence as a distinct people was doubtful? Writing of this terrible tension between altruistically connecting to others while protecting your own identity and your own boundaries is what makes the Jewish prophets stand out among the Axial Age innovators and what makes them relevant to us today. In our present highly interconnected world, we are likewise caught between empathizing with our fellow humans and worrying about our own self-interests. The prophets addressed this dilemma by constructing a story that promised a magnificent future, no matter what was happening in the present. Their story of hope was modified and tweaked over time, but still remains on many levels with us today.

Engaging the Jewish prophets, we are challenged to reach for their spiritual treasures while defending against the noxious parts of the teachings and values that can be found in their stories. Who would not want to be more courageous, insightful, and articulate? Yet sometimes the enthusiasm and charisma of one who claims the prophet's mantle can hide destructive forces that emerge over time. The agnostic is challenged to embrace Axial Age insights while identifying and confronting the more harmful elements in their stories. Just how to do that will be addressed in the remaining chapters.

The Jewish prophets of the sixth century had an earlier model, the ninth-century prophet Elijah. His story is found in the *Book of Kings* and is overlaid with legend and miracles. Nevertheless, for Jewish and, to a lesser extent, Christian traditions, he remains especially significant. He not only left his imprint on those traditions, but he also helped define an understanding of what a prophet should look like. On the other hand, he does not always give an example of a highly ethical life, as will be shown in the next chapter.

2

Elijah: The Once and Future Prophet

The prophet is a man who feels fiercely ... God is raging in the prophet's words.

—ABRAHAM HESCHEL, *THE PROPHETS*

THE STORY OF ELIJAH gives us a larger-than-life protagonist who still features prominently in Jewish folklore. Although he does not have a book named after him, he became the model for what a prophet should be. Historically, he emerged in the middle of the ninth century BCE in the kingdom of Samaria (see map below). Samaria and its Southern sister kingdom Judah were once thought to be part of Solomon's mythical empire, now divided into two after his death. The two kingdoms enjoyed some independence because Assyria, an eventual superpower, had not yet exerted control over the region.

In the time of Elijah, Samaria, also called Israel, was ruled by the powerful Omride dynasty and was the first Jewish kingdom to be mentioned in contemporaneous writings outside Samaria and Judah. Elijah is inspired by Yahweh, one of several deities then known to the people of the two sister kingdoms, to denounce this dynasty, including King Ahab and his wife Jezebel, for its preference of another god over Yahweh.

Living before the universal Axial Age prophets of the sixth century, Elijah has a limited scope: his concern is with one particular dynasty and the one particular objective of moving worship of Yahweh to the highest status. Armed with such focused intensity, Elijah introduces a level of violence while pursuing his objective that by today's standards would be punished as war crimes. Nevertheless, for better or worse, Elijah becomes a model for the later prophets of the Axial Age.

Elijah: The Once and Future Prophet

What Makes Elijah So Special?

The story of Elijah is an artificially constructed one. His story is marked by legends, such as the time he parted the Jordan River. However, the legends are probably plagiarized from his supposed successor, Elisha. "The Elisha stories served as the source for the Elijah narratives. Originally, both men have nothing to do with each other, they merely represented the same type of a man of God," states a leading commentator on the Jewish prophets, Richard Kratz.[1]

One reason why Elijah emerges as the premier prophet (not only for the Northern Kingdom, but for the Southern one as well) is due to one episode in his story that clearly separates him—not only from Elisha, but from any other prophet, king, or holy person in the Jewish Scriptures. The Bible claims that Elijah did not die, but was taken bodily into heaven: a chariot and horses of fire came down "and Elijah ascended in a whirlwind into heaven" (2 Kgs 2:11).[2]

The legend of Elijah's ascension was seen as absolute proof that he was a true prophet. However, such a one-off event also reveals the problem, if not dilemma, of how to recognize a true prophet. The books of Kings hint at this difficulty because different prophets tell the ruling monarchs different things. For example, one Jewish prophet is right on one score, but wrong on another, and gets killed by a bear. Later on, the question of who is a true prophet became critical for the ruling elite, especially of the Southern Kingdom of Judah.

Looking at a map in which the kingdoms of Samaria and Judah are part of a larger region gives context for their concern (see map below). In his book *Guns, Germs, and Steel*, Jared Diamond argues that kingdoms located near the Tigris and Euphrates Rivers (modern-day Iraq) had certain advantages in the ancient world. Eventually they used these advantages to expand their borders and to conquer neighboring kingdoms. Around the time of Elijah, one

---

1. Kratz, *Prophets of Israel*, 23.
2. All Scripture quotes taken from New Revised Standard Version.

such kingdom, Assyria, began to exert itself against the smaller kingdoms to its west.

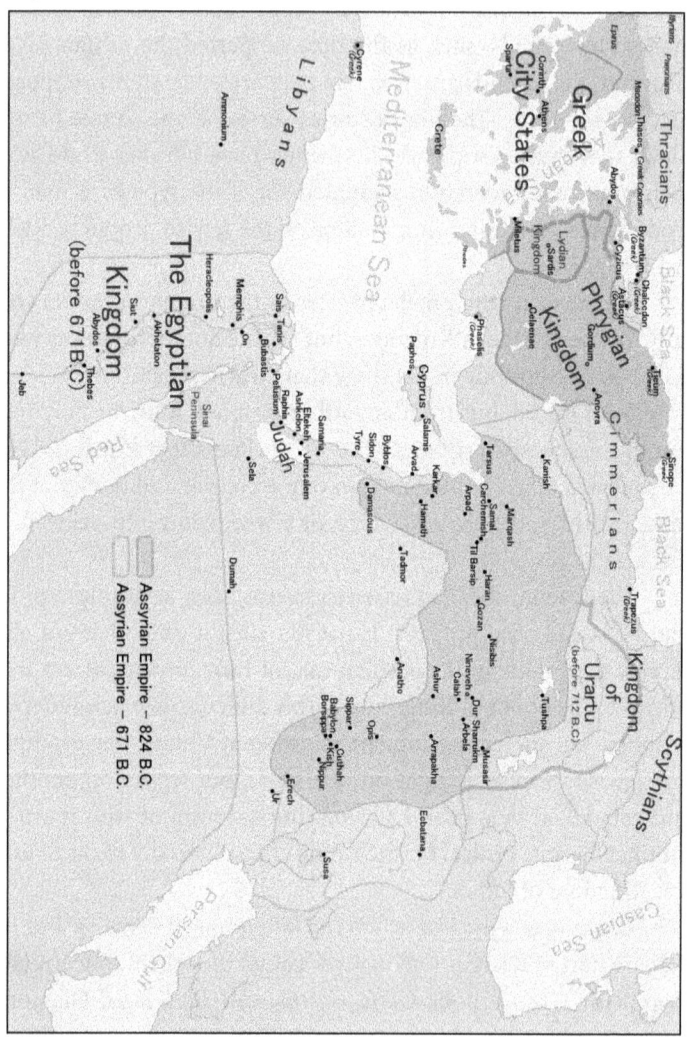

At first these smaller kingdoms joined together to push back against invaders or seek help from Egypt, the other superpower of the day. However, this strategy did not work for Samaria. Roughly one hundred years after Elijah, in 722 BCE, Samaria was conquered. But that wasn't all—many people, including the ruling

Elijah: The Once and Future Prophet

elite, were sent to previously conquered countries while people from other countries were sent to live in what was once Samaria. Samaria no longer existed as independent people with their own king. The identity of this once-strong kingdom was diluted when it was absorbed into the powerful Assyrian empire. Its Jewish people mingled with other races and were later on considered "impure" by religious Jews of the Southern Kingdom.

After Samaria's destruction, the ruling elite of Judah worried about their survival because the superpowers of the time, Assyria and Egypt, wanted to control all the smaller kingdoms for political and economic reasons. Caught between the two, a small kingdom like Judah had to decide whose side to be on. To make matters worse, the tides of war shifted, with sometimes Assyria on top and other times Egypt. Judah's rulers and religious leaders likely thought of Elijah as a true prophet and therefore a possible key to their deliberations to seek a safe path in perilous times.

Not surprisingly, the scribes of Judah wrote the story of Elijah into their own histories, even though these histories were written long after Samaria had been destroyed. The scribes who wrote down the stories were interpreting the history of Samaria like tea leaves to try to understand what happened in the North so as to prevent a similar disaster in their Southern Kingdom. They believed that Samaria was destroyed because the people did not put aside their idols and worship Yahweh alone. The scribes of Judah had discovered an insurance policy: while their kingdom might be destroyed because of their idol worship, they could still survive as a people by a mass conversion to Yahweh alone.

These Southern scribes likely overlooked Elijah's bloody modus operandi because they took for granted that Samaria was a violent kingdom. In the two hundred years of its history, it was ruled by some nine dynasties, each making it a point to destroy any competitors from the previous one. In their retelling, Elijah is a prophet who told the people of Samaria how they could have acted to prevent such a tragedy. He becomes a model for future prophets in Judah who were also worried about their kingdom's survival. They glamorized Elijah's life story through miraculous feats and portrayed him as the essence of what a prophet should be.

Elijah's Violent Acts

When fifty soldiers come to take him to see Ahaziah, another king from the Omride dynasty, the prophet calls upon heaven to send down fire and destroys all of them. He also destroys a second contingent from the king likewise dispatched to confront him. Finally, the leader of a third contingent senses that he had better be careful and simply asks the prophet's permission to accompany him to see the king. Elijah is not threatened by this request and agrees to accompany him to the meeting with Ahaziah, which goes well. Why did he resort to such violence in the first place?

Elijah's bloodiest deed was likely the afternoon Yahweh inspired him to kill 450 prophets of a rival religion. Elijah and these other prophets had a face-off to see which of their gods could set fire to the sacrificial altars each camp had set up. The other prophets failed. Adding insult to injury, Elijah drenched his wooden altar with water before he called down fire on the sacrifice, which burned it up. Not satisfied with such a resounding victory, he ordered the assembled people to grab hold of all these prophets and not let anyone escape. The Scriptures casually state: "Elijah brought them down to the Wadi Kishon and killed them there" (1 Kgs 18:40).

Elijah is implicated in other murders as well. He recognizes Jehu, the leader of a coup against the Omride dynasty, as the legitimate king. As was customary, this usurper then went on a rampage, killing all the heirs to the previous dynasty and thereby eliminating the competition while he formed a new dynasty. The Scriptures justify this behavior: "[he wiped them out] according to the word of the Lord that Yahweh spoke to Elijah" (2 Kgs 10:17). Jehu also massacres the prophets of Baal, as did Elijah. In fact, the killing spree goes on until, the Scriptures tell us, only seven thousand people are left in the kingdom who had not worshiped Baal.

Elijah's Non-Violent Side

The bloodthirsty parts of Elijah's story are nearly blotted out by a number of legendary good deeds and miracles: he replenished the widow's handful of meal and a jug of oil and so continuously supplied food for himself, the widow, and her son; furthermore, when her son died, he revived him (1 Kgs, 17:15-24); he lives for forty days and nights with only a cake and a jar of water for sustenance (1 Kgs 19:5-8); ravens brought him bread and meat twice a day when he escaped to the desert (1 Kgs 17:6); his prayer ended a disastrous drought in the kingdom: when there was no cloud on the horizon, Elijah accurately predicted that rain was coming (1 Kgs 18:43-45).

Predicting the future became the hallmark of the true prophet, as well. In addition to rainfall, Elijah predicted the death of Ahab and Jezebel. Yet it is in Elijah's trials and tribulations that we see the essence of the prophet's vocation. On the run from Jezebel's fury, he escaped into the desert, where he thought he would die. He followed his call zealously even though he thought the cause was hopeless. He was obedient even if it meant his own death.

Elijah's courage and persistence was fueled by his intimate relationship with his god, which is described at one of the prophet's low points. Elijah was a hunted man and fearful that, despite his zealous service to Yahweh, he would soon be captured and executed. Ever obedient, he answers the call to approach the entrance to the cave where he is hiding. This time Yahweh comes to him not in wind, earthquake, or fire, but in a still, small voice. The prophet is then given instructions to anoint rulers who would then unleash their fury upon those in Samaria who worship another god.

The Elijah story embodies the warring sides of his religious beliefs. On the one hand, the displays of violence and murder are a natural consequence of any religion that claims its deity is supreme and needs to be acknowledged as such. With such a premise, its adherents will view other belief systems as an insult or even a threat to their deity. Members can be emboldened to discriminate against or even persecute such perceived enemies in the self-righteous claim that they are doing their god's bidding.

On the other hand, parts of the Elijah story proclaim the merciful kindness of Yahweh and the concern for justice toward the poor and marginalized. Additionally, they model the self-sacrifice of a true man of God, who suffers greatly for his belief. And finally, the prophet has a special calling, a connection to the transcendent that empowers him to do good deeds and to fight for justice. Elijah models a religion that can be both a curse and a blessing. Not only does such duality continue in history, but its representative, Elijah, would do so also.

The Return of Elijah

In addition to solidifying his credentials as a true prophet, Elijah's ascension imbued future prophets with the hope of a happy ending. As Yahweh saved Elijah, so also would their god ultimately save the Jewish people. Even after Judah was destroyed and the reign of Davidic kings ended, hope would remain; over the centuries, Jewish writers often wondered when Elijah would return. Elijah transcended history to become a symbol of Yahweh's promise to restore the nation.

The book of the prophet Malachi completes the Jewish Scriptures, at least in the arrangement decided by Christians. The last words of this last book read: "Lo, I will send you the prophet Elijah before the great and terrible day of the Lord comes. He will turn the hearts of parents to their children and the hearts of children to their parents, so I will not come and strike the land with a curse"(Mal 4:5–6).

The bringer of violence was transformed into a bringer of blessing. He becomes a magical character in Jewish folklore. "Little children love him because he is an invisible guest at the Passover Seder, when he is supposed to slip into the house to taste the wine from a special ceremonial cup set aside for him, known as Elijah's

Elijah: The Once and Future Prophet

cup. A special chair called Elijah's chair is set up for him at the circumcision ceremony. At the end of the Sabbath he is invoked with a special song. And, most importantly, he is believed to be the one who will arrive on earth to announce the coming of the Messiah, the son of David."[3]

Elijah's Mixed Messages

The story of Elijah in the book of Kings is described as one of the most brilliant and compelling narratives in the entire Bible.[4] However, the power of the story can blind us to its mixed messages and unanswered questions of morality. These difficulties happen when the prophetic story with its descriptions of visionary experiences meets the complicated demands of political and cultural life. Later prophets faced these difficulties as they brought their insights to bear in the complicated times in which they found themselves. For example:

If you are so powerful, why don't you do something? In the story, Yahweh is so powerful that he can destroy hundreds of people and justify the slaughter of thousands. The more substantial the claims made for Yahweh—he is the Creator of the world and the Lord of history—the more pressure on this protagonist to do something commensurate with his capacities. Elijah tells of the deeds of such a powerful god, but later writers had a more nuanced view and played down fantastic divine interventions, relegating them to a mythical past or predicting their appearance in a hoped-for future.

Still, the dilemma remained. The promised future did not always make sense when the real world evidenced injustice, tragedy, and harm done to decent people. Sometimes described as the problem of evil, the challenge is how to justify a just god in an unjust world. Elijah foreshadows the story of Job in the sense that Elijah's experience of the transcendent supports him during times of struggle. He holds on to his belief; he stays on the path he was

3. Schreiber, *Hearing the Voice*, 13.
4. Millgram, *Elijah Enigma*, 16.

inspired to follow, and is comforted in his religious experience. The prophets would be sustained by their visions, but questions remained for followers who had trouble believing in the promised future.

Who is God's Anointed?

Elijah turned against Ahab, but he would embrace Jehu. It was as though an intervening god necessitated an intervening human who would get things done. Later prophets would often bank on a particular ruler or a class of people as the ones to lead the way. Power struggles became endemic as different prophets supported different factions. In fact, the history of Samaria showed just how impotent Yahweh was when it came to the real world of politics. The Elijah-supported coup of Jehu brought little change to that Northern Kingdom. Religiously, the evolution toward monotheism stalled and, politically, one dynasty replaced another in bloody coups until the Assyrians destroyed the kingdom.

However, the hope for some concrete expression of Yahweh's power did not go away. Religious individuals would "see" the hand of their god in the movement of history and in the winners and losers of battles. It is tempting to see this need to embrace powerful leaders and discover confirming meaning in events as simply the projection of our own primordial desires for security. We can blind ourselves to the violence and corruption of leaders we have ordained as our saviors.

Tolerance or Intolerance?

For Elijah, belief in Yahweh became a touchstone that determined who was in and who was out. The worshipers of Baal were clearly out, but why were they slaughtered? How can a religious-based cleansing of one's own people be explained? Part of it may have been that Elijah was part of a persecuted minority who sought vengeance when the tables were turned. Part of it may have been

Elijah: The Once and Future Prophet

the need to support a leader who promised to protect these once discriminated-against people. What is striking is that the vengeance is done in their god's name. It is as though their god has given the message that he is so insulted by a less flattering view of himself that he declares that those holding it have lost their right to exist.

Future Jewish prophets struggled to make their message more universal, but they had to overcome the terrible intolerance of the Elijah story. The more advanced of them dreamed of a time in which warring enemies became friends because they recognized Yahweh's power and desire for peace among the nations. Their solutions were awkward because they faced a dilemma: how to form a chosen people under Yahweh while maintaining a more tolerant view toward those who are not of his realm. Rather than look at their story too closely or critically, believers glossed over the difficult parts. That is what happened with Elijah. In the book of Malachi, Elijah became the symbol of a more kindly view of his religion, one in which the fate of those who did not belong to it was sidestepped.

Engaging the Elijah Story

To engage the story of Elijah is to recognize that the story is still played out today in various degrees of violence. Elijah's call for the kingdom of Yahweh is echoed in similar calls for a Christian nation or an Islamic caliphate. The demand for religious purity can celebrate violence as a tool to achieve its ends. In fact, violence in one form or another is seen as necessary and even a sign of one's commitment to the cause.

As in the case of Elijah, the violence is often accompanied by promises of security or of future well-being. Additionally, a religion can distract us from its violent side by offering spiritual goods such as concern for others, an experience of community, and the comfort of ritual. Appreciating that religion does good things can seduce us into rationalizing blatant or subtle forms of violence, which can be camouflaged as sinfulness, deadly conformity, or crippling obedience. Here is one small example.

The entrance rite at the church I attend is focused on sinfulness. We are encouraged to metaphorically prostrate ourselves before God and admit the errors of our ways and the harm we have done to others. We call on our merciful God to take away our sins. Two problems. First of all, this seemingly innocuous opening rite identifies us as characters in the middle section of the prophets' story. We have fallen through sinning and await a final resolution in the future. From a psychological perspective, participating in that rite emphasizes our weakness and tends to damage our self-esteem.

Not believing in the story, but joining in a search for the transcendent, an agnostic is able to push back against such a self-harming storyline and instead evoke a different kind of feeling, thereby creating a different kind of experience. As argued in a later chapter, the common spiritual experience for theists and non-theists alike is awe. We are awed by the beauty and majesty of our world and by the mystery of our own life. Religious practice offers the opportunity to separate ourselves from our day-to-day world and take time to experience, even briefly, something of the transcendent. We hope not for absolution for our sins or a resolution of intractable problems, but rather insight into how we can continue to evolve as individuals, while working to build on the Axial Age concerns for the evolution of our species.

The Elijah story is awe-inspiring. He vanishes foes, works miracles, and is taken to heaven when his work is done. He lives on in Jewish legends and makes a guest appearance in the gospel story about Jesus. An agnostic tempers such an overwhelming presentation by remembering those facts that make Elijah something of a false prophet. He glorifies violence when it is done in the name of his god; he breaks down the barrier between church and state by making divine claims for an earthly ruler; he dehumanizes and demonizes those with different beliefs. A close reading of the Elijah story warns us to be careful of prophets. We are advised to scrutinize the stories they tell and the claims they make.

Elijah: The Once and Future Prophet

The legends and heaven-sent violence in the Elijah story clearly demonstrate that we are dealing with story and not history. The accounts of future prophets will claim to be historical, and to some degree they are. Yet despite the historical overlay future prophets are telling the same story. Remembering the story of Elijah helps an agnostic to investigate carefully any truth claims or derived practices, such as the penitential rite, stemming from the narrative. Thoughtfully questioning the story is like donning a psycho-spiritual hazmat suit that protects a person while allowing that person to invest in the awe-inspiring search for transcendence. Protectively engaged, a person can be open to experiences that offer insight and the motivation to travel our own path toward an uncertain future.

A century after Elijah, a prophet who was both humble and an outsider begins his mission in a still unconquered Samaria. He also questions what he was doing, which put his life at risk. However, this prophet broke away dramatically from the Elijah tradition by projecting Yahweh's violent actions into the future. He also becomes the first to be found outside the Bible's historical writings. Amos was the first prophet to have his own book.

3

Amos: The Prophet of Justice

Is God an example of justice, or justice an example of God? Does it matter?

John Caputo, *The Prayers and Tears of Jacques Derrida*

The first thing you notice about the city of San Francisco's monument to Martin Luther King Jr. is the waterfall. A continuous stream of water pours over a man-made cliff about fifty feet wide and two stories high. As you get closer you can see the path leading behind the waterfall to a wall inscribed with various excerpts from speeches by Dr. King. The wall also contains one of Dr. King's favorite quotes, which probably inspired the artist who developed the monument. The quote, which King included in his magnificent "I Have a Dream" speech, delivered in Washington, DC in 1963, is from the prophet Amos: "But let justice roll down like waters and righteousness like an ever-flowing stream" (Amos 5:24).[1]

This freighted phrase provides insight into the three major and disparate accomplishments of the prophet Amos. His concern for justice helped him become the first Hebrew prophet whose

1. All following biblical citations are from the book of Amos.

Amos: The Prophet of Justice

words were written in a stand-alone document instead of being placed in a history book, such as in the case with Elijah. Second, it places him as a harbinger of the Axial Age because Amos introduces something transcendent that has serious implications for daily living. Finally, the notions of justice and the concern for injustice mark Amos as a truly modern prophet.

A Realistic Prophet

A century after Elijah, prophets moved from having supporting roles in the history books to becoming main characters in the books named after them. Amos, a Judean, prophesying about the Northern Kingdom of Samaria, was the first one to break the bonds of legend and portray a more realistic version of a man obsessed with fulfilling a call given to him by Yahweh. Gone are the bursts of fire from the sky to destroy enemies or the miraculous powers to raise the dead or feed a widow. Instead, Amos presents himself as a simple man, a shepherd and dresser of sycamore trees, who comes from a small town near Bethlehem, in the Southern Kingdom of Judah.

He makes no claims to be trained as a prophet but rather claims his authority comes from an unexpected vision from Yahweh. His task is to warn the people of the Northern Kingdom of Samaria that they are doomed because of their sinful behavior, for which they will be destroyed and sent into exile. The book of Amos ends with a promise of restoration but was likely written centuries later as a consolation to the people of Judea, who were also defeated and sent into exile.

Like many prophets that followed him, Amos was an outsider who claimed authority by virtue of a special calling by Yahweh. His outsider status gave him the perspective to criticize what he saw as a betrayal of the commitments he believed people had made to Yahweh in a distant Golden Age. Unlike Elijah, Amos did not focus on people's special worship activities, but on specific, mundane acts of daily living, which he saw as immoral and terribly harmful. Amos saw a society in which the rich were growing richer by marginalizing the less fortunate. He lambasted the wealthy for oppressing the poor and crushing the needy (4:1). He claimed that their greed had infected their judicial system so that the poor did not get a fair hearing (5:12). Amaziah, the king's own prophet, was incensed by Amos's declarations since overall things were good for the people of Samaria: the kingdom was expanding and becoming more powerful as a player in the politics of the Middle East.

So what was wrong? Samaria had become wealthy enough to support its own army, thereby gaining importance as a member in political alliances as well as becoming economically sophisticated, making it a valuable trading partner. This wealth was a function of an economy that depended on large-scale farms, as well as a central and powerful bureaucracy to manage the trade, support the army, and conduct alliances. However, the ever-increasing need for large-scale farms to provide specific crops for export and the cost of a bigger government put pressure on the smaller farmers who became exploited by the more powerful landowners.[2]

While such economic and political tumult was taking place, the main religious establishment, which was polytheistic, supported the changes. Breaking with the establishment, Amos responded to these changes by invoking a special god, Yahweh, whom he claimed objected to the injustices that accompanied newfound wealth and power. His theological justification was essentially a narrative that argued for a return to an earlier, mythical time when Yahweh had established a more egalitarian society. He preached about a Golden Age in which traditional values and small landowners set the standards for a god-fearing society. Amos held a minority theological position, even though Jewish Scriptures might lead us to think otherwise. He was part of the Yahweh-alone movement, which might anachronistically be called a conservative movement that invoked the values of an earlier time to critique current behavior.

---

2. Premnath, *Eighth Century Prophets*, 7–24.

Amos: The Prophet of Justice

His Narrative

Amos describes a three-part story composed of:

1. A Golden Age when people lived just lives.
2. A time of rampant injustice, that eventually led to the punishing reaction of Yahweh for immoral behavior.
3. A restoration to another, even better, Golden Age.

What is significant about this mythical narrative is its emphasis on justice as the basis for right living. In the earlier period before they had kings or rulers, the people lived justly, primarily because of what Yahweh had done for them. Later on, they "forgot" this early part of their story and began to exploit one another, which led to intense punishment because Yahweh is so intimately tied into the transcendent value of justice that he becomes mightily offended by what he sees.

The god that Amos describes has the credentials to back up his complaints. Yahweh is both the source of creation and the determiner of history. He has done and will do things out of a profound sense of justice. Amos introduces the idea of the day of the Lord as a time of ultimate reckoning for sinners. "It is darkness not light; as if someone fled from a lion, and was met by a bear; or went into the house and rested a hand against the wall and was bitten by a snake" (5:19). Amos goes on to prophesy that their involvement in the cult of Yahweh will not save them. Using hyperbole, he has Yahweh declare that worship without just behavior is worthless: " I hate, I despise your festivals, and I take no delight in your solemn assemblies" (5:21).

However, Samaria would not be the only nation to be destroyed. The book of Amos opens with four chapters of describing blistering violence against other cities and states: Damascus, Gaza, Tyre, Moab, and even the Southern Kingdom of Judah. The retaliation is so brutal and extensive that the modern reader would likely grow numb or skip over the verses and chapters that describe these graphic and humiliating punishments. Later prophets continue this two-step process of excruciatingly painful punishment followed by promised redemption.

How can Yahweh be so angry? Jewish philosopher Abraham Heschel reframed Yahweh's intense feelings as an important insight into Jewish theology. He argued that the Jewish Scriptures tell of a god who is so involved in the world as to be affected by human behavior. This is a God who actually cares about what we do and by so doing elevates emotions to a spiritual level—feelings matter. He argues that it is the prophetic tradition, with its description of a suffering and caring God, which establishes this novel sense of the divine. "At the heart of the prophetic affirmation is the certainty that God is concerned about the world."[3] This passionate concern for the world also made the story memorable. This God cared for his people and essentially promised a happy ending.

The story begun by Amos gives another theological insight. Yahweh does so much because he is the god of both creation and history. He is the one who made the stars and turns the darkness into morning (5:8–9). He is the also the one who enters history to retaliate with vengeful destruction. Later, the prophet Isaiah would develop this insight into the novel idea that Yahweh was the only God. The Yahweh-alone movement evolved into the one God of all.

Amos, Harbinger of the Axial Age

Behind the story begun by Amos was the Axial Age sensitivity that heaven and earth are to be consistent. It is only by aligning ourselves with some transcendent value that we grow into what we are supposed to be. The moral of his story is that we are to be godlike. For Amos, the main divine characteristic is the transcendent value of justice. He preached that following the worship and rituals that celebrated Yahweh would bring people closer to the ideal, just as Plato hoped reason would. Arguably, Amos is describing an awakening toward the goal of harmonious living similar to the awakenings described by Buddha and Confucius.

3. Heschel, *Prophets*, 39

Amos: The Prophet of Justice

The story told by Amos was also a universal story. While Israel and Judah at times had special status, their god was for all people. The prophet has Yahweh declaring that other peoples like the Ethiopians, Philistines, and Aramaeans were also part of his plan (9:7). Amos touches on a theme that not only future prophets but all of us struggle with, especially today: how to celebrate one's identity (religious, tribal, political), and at the same time value people who are different.

Later prophets expanded on this theme, insisting that the Jews were to be a light to the gentiles, a model for the holiness and right behavior they had developed with Yahweh's help. The whole world was to be influenced in a positive manner. Amos began the movement that reflected what Karl Jaspers called the "step into universality" that marked the Axial Age.[4]

In answering his prophetic call, Amos found the courage to follow the beliefs that put him in harm's way. Equally important, he found in his own visions the criteria to evaluate his world and his place in it. In that courageous evaluation he saw what no one else did: striving for wealth led to destructive greed and the amassing of wealth led to inequality. The rising power of Samaria led to the oppression of many of its people. Samaria was in a death spiral.

If Amos were more like a present day op-ed writer, he would have predicted that increased wealth only made Samaria more attractive to the growing superpower of the day. Whether they came from Egypt or Mesopotamia, empires made it their business to increase wealth from neighboring countries in much the same way Samaritan elite were draining small farmers of their livelihoods. However, Amos was a theologian, not a political analyst, and while his concept of a just god who wanted all people to live in holiness and justice brought him closer to the thinkers of the Axial Age, this same god set Amos apart from them.

---

4. Jaspers, *Origin*, 2.

The Problem with Yahweh

In the story begun by Amos, universal justice could only come from his god. God had to make sure it happened; otherwise, heaven and earth would be out of sync. Furthermore, to make it happen he had to intervene—to both punish and reward in a way that left no doubt. Such promises of divine intervention could not be sustained. Later writers tried to shore up failed predictions by offering excuses or putting off the intervention further into the future. Over time, different voices offered differing views.

The overdependence on Yahweh was the real problem. The search for a divine intervention overshadowed the need for human ones. A grand solution minimized the importance of partial ones. While Amos was concerned with worldly problems and individual responsibility—"Seek good and not evil that you may live" (5:14)—the positing of an intervening God established an overreliance on authority. In contrast, Buddha resisted the pull of would-be disciples for answers from on high. He held and taught that people found answers for right living by disciplined introspection.[5]

A second problem with the vision of Amos, which was carried over to the later Jewish prophets, is that they overinvested in the future. The prophet's message would be evaluated on the ability to foretell the future. It would become the major criteria for evaluating who was a true or false prophet. The dilemma here is that one cannot evaluate a prophet in the present. By default, the attractiveness of the predictions and the charisma of the predictor will likely establish credibility. Centuries later, at the time of Jesus, there were many false prophets who led people into disastrous encounters with their Roman overlords.

Amos gained special status because he foretold that the kingdom of Samaria would be destroyed, which actually happened in 722 BCE, a few years after the prophet's prediction. His promise of restoration would give hope to the people in the Southern Kingdom of Judah, who likewise experienced destruction and exile years later. When that promise was not fulfilled and prophets

---

5. Armstrong, *Transformation*, 286.

began to lose favor, the words of Amos that spoke out against injustice and inauthentic worship still had value. His hope for a highly moral society that reflected his god's plan for humankind continues to resonate, even today.

Amos, a Prophet for Today

The book's vision has continued to inspire. He critiqued the economic system of his day, called *latifundialization*, meaning the accumulation of land by the wealthy elite, which led to the deprivation of the peasantry.[6] Amos has emerged as a resource and inspiration for social activists and liberation theologians who likewise speak truth to power as they critique social ills tied to a changing economy that greatly favors the rich and leaves so many poor people adrift.[7] This challenge to power is what distinguishes the Israelite prophets from those in neighboring cultures.

At the time of Amos, prophets were attached to the king and would be asked for advice when the king faced a decision, such as whether or not to go to war. In contrast, this Israelite prophet attacked the king and his powerful supporters not only by challenging the prevalent economic system and the cult (of which the king was the head), but also by predicting that the wrath of Yahweh would be directed toward him and his kingdom. In retaliation, a priest complained to the king that Amos had conspired against him and should be exiled from the land. In response, Amos boldly declared that Israel would go into exile (7:10; 7:17).

Engaging the Amos Story

Engaging the Amos story means appreciating the power of the call to justice. Amos served as an inspiration to the modern prophet Martin Luther King Jr., who identified with Amos's prophetic role. We have King's own vision that he might not reach the promised

6. Premnath, *Eighth Century Prophets*, 1.
7. Mein, "Radical Amos," 117–40.

land, but believed that the promises would come true. Such a vision is consistent with the hope for a better future found in the book of Amos. The faith of prophets like Amos and Martin Luther King Jr. for a more just world sustained them in the face of setbacks and continued injustice.

Others, both religious and secular, have also worked to achieve a more humane society at great personal cost and even continued despite the pain of defeat. Activist Dorothy Day championed justice for the poor and homeless in a society and culture that tolerated their persecution and would become even more materialistic and militaristic over the years. Environmentalist Ken Saro-Wiwa would battle the oil companies that exploited his home country of Nigeria and seduced its government; he was eventually executed on trumped-up charges.

The battle for justice continues as individuals spend or sacrifice their lives to bring about a more just world. Is it possible that the evolutionary breakthrough reached in the Axial Age has so embedded itself in our consciousness that the dream of a just world will not die? In particular, will the example of prophets like Amos remain a source of inspiration, not only for past generations, but also for present and future ones as well? Or is it that the idea of justice itself is so embedded in our imaginations that when a prophetic figure articulates its absence we instinctively realize our need to act?

Philosopher Jacques Derrida elevated justice to a near transcendental status, identifying it as synonymous with his concept of deconstruction, his insatiable process of closely scrutinizing claims to truth. Justice was the wellspring that motivated him to challenge the ideologies that papered over their contradictions and inconsistencies, as well as to point out the terrible injustices most of us skimmed over and ultimately ignored. He claimed that deconstruction is justice and imagined an infinite and never-ending process that called all people to work in a concerted effort to push back against injustice in all its forms.[8]

---

8. Weber, "Deconstruction," 179–84.

Amos: The Prophet of Justice

Although a philosopher, Jacques Derrida searched for transcendent justice rather than absolute truth because he believed that all serious truth claims can be oppressive and unjust. He reminds us that justice is found not only in acting fairly, but also in thinking clearly. Amos tells a story in which his god is the main character, but then claims the story is history; it really happened that way. Amos and the prophets that followed him make a category mistake: story and history are separate domains. The truth claims of a character in a story can only be validated by evidence outside that narrative, for example, from science.

Amos lived almost three thousand years before the science arrived that challenged the historical roots, and therefore the truth claims, of his story. However, today's religious and spiritual individuals have no such excuse. If they ignore the role scientific investigation can play in understanding their beliefs, they become victims to the oppressive ideology and unjust practices sanctioned by the story they claim to be history.

Derrida's insistence on deconstructing ideology is somewhat similar to that of an agnostic, one who searches for the transcendent but is skeptical about truth claims, especially those that demand allegiance because a character in a story—even if he is called God—declared them to be true. An agnostic engages with the religious story to distinguish those spiritual values and insights stemming from a religious experience from the oppressive ideology that justifies injustice. The hope is to be so inspired by this engagement that one is motivated to recognize injustice and work to lessen it by critical thinking and right action.

Amos acted in a similar fashion when he confronted a society and culture that accepted as normal the marginalization of many. Amos traced injustice to an abandonment of traditional values and to an empty worship service. When he identified a way of thinking that normalized systematic oppression, he based his critique upon an imaginary past. Was he right for the wrong reasons? Or is justice such an unattainable objective that we create some near-absolute source of power to help us take on such an overwhelming project as injustice?

What we can say is that his religious experiences enabled Amos to stand apart from his culture and speak out against behavior he saw as harmful and destructive. While we might object to his solution and prescription for change, we can admire his courage, as well as his trust in something larger than himself. What that something is remains a matter for discussion. The real promise of prophets like Amos and other spokespersons of the Axial Age is that there is something we can call on to give strength and guidance in times of crisis.

4

Ezekiel: A Cautionary Tale

Whatever functions to hold our life together is our religion.

JOHN NAVONE, *SEEKING GOD IN STORY*

THE BOOK OF EZEKIEL presents the prophet as living on the borderland between creativity and madness. Scripture scholars see this story as offering new perspectives on the Jewish religion including, as one author states, a strikingly original cosmic vision of god working in the world that is "unattested elsewhere."[1] Another group of scholars describes him as deranged and delusional, a psychotic who gives readers glimpses of pornographic violence. Underlying Ezekiel's mixture of originality and pathology is a thinly disguised authoritarianism that asks for total obedience. It is tempting to think of the prophet's call for an authoritarian regime as simply a reflection of his desperate need for structure that could regulate both his brilliance and compromised mental health.

Psychological theorizing aside, Ezekiel's vision of the transcendent is so infused with the power of Yahweh and the prophet's own need for a stable identity that the sense of justice, begun with

---

1. Boccaccini, *Roots*, 303.

the prophet Amos, is nearly lost. Instead, he gives us a god so powerful that there is little room for human participation: people are practically excused from the hard work of engaging the transcendent to solve real life issues. Instead, Ezekiel gives us a god that will take care of everything, but at the cost of imposing his will upon the people and overwhelming them with divine interventions. Ezekiel's story begins with a religious experience that transforms him and legitimates his call to prophesy.

The Call

In the first verses of the book, the thirty-year-old priest Ezekiel is standing by the Chebar River in Babylon when the heavens open up and he hears the word of his god. In a theophany more familiar to neighboring pagan religions than Jewish Scriptures,[2] Yahweh's call is accompanied by four creatures, each with four heads; wheels within wheels; the sounds of thunder; and a flaming throne of amber and sapphire. From the midst of these fantastic images booms the divine voice that commissions him to reach out to his fellow exiles. Because his task would be so difficult and his fellow exiles so reluctant to listen to him, the Lord makes him eat the scroll on which his message was written. Scholars see this action as a metaphor that justifies and privileges the written word over the spoken one. From a psychological perspective, it also serves as an anchoring solution for the prophet who must struggle, not only with external threats, but also with the weight of his incredible vision—he now has a script to follow.

Ezekiel's vision at the River Chebar is also an example of the prophet's creativity. He has borrowed from ancient Middle Eastern symbols, images, and motifs, and used them to structure a degree of "literary coherence unmatched in the biblical canon."[3] In particular, he uses material from the cultures of countries to which Jews were exiled in order to better gain their attention. He attempts to establish his credibility and authority by implicitly

2. Peterson, *Ezekiel*, 107.
3. Odell, *Ezekiel*, 1.

Ezekiel: A Cautionary Tale

claiming that Yahweh is speaking to him in the symbols of their Babylonian captors.

The call is also a frightening burden. The prophet is given the thankless task of speaking to the people even though they may not care to listen. Faced with such a tough audience, Ezekiel carries out his responsibilities in ways both mundane and bizarre. He acts out the coming destruction of Jerusalem by lying on his left side for a specific number of days, then turning onto the right side for another period (4:4–8),[4] and rations out his food to demonstrate what it would be like for the citizens of Jerusalem under siege (4:9–17). He goes even further and states that this destruction is warranted because of the people's wickedness, since this wickedness surpassed that of all the other nations. He identifies the source of this wickedness as their failure to keep the covenant established with their god Yahweh in the desert. He essentially draws a parallel between the breaking of the people's covenant with Yahweh with the breaking of their king's covenant with the ruler of Babylon—the terror unleashed by the Babylonian armies is simultaneously Yahweh's punishment of his wicked people.

An Imposing God

The god revealed in the call will impose his will on his people, just as, in the opening chapter of the Bible, Yahweh imposed his will on chaos to create the world. In the book of Ezekiel, the primary imposition is punishment. In two controversial sections, chapters 16 and 23, women representing Judah and Samaria are tortured in scenes of pornographic violence. Yet, after the violence comes a promised blessing. Yahweh declares that the two kingdoms will be reunited on some future date, like two sticks joined together (37:15–23).

The prophet berates the people for their sins on behalf of their god. The words he uses (such as "pollution") connote not just moral violation, but additionally, scholars have noted, a basic disorder needing to be righted—like chaos in the book of Genesis. In the

4. All biblical references are from the book of Ezekiel.

example of the metaphorical stories of the two women mentioned previously, it is not simply the women's sins that are condemned. It is *they* who are out of order—i.e., they were acting aggressively like men instead of passively like women. Likewise, all those in authority are berated for having neglected their duties, like shepherds who have abandoned their flocks—the weak are not strengthened, the sick not healed, the strayed not sought after (34:1–10).

In order to bring back order, Yahweh essentially does away with the kingship. He becomes the good shepherd, the true ruler, while the sheep-like people are rescued and cared for. Ezekiel goes on to indict all the so-called leaders who have not done their duty: "In effect, Ezekiel eliminates the entire leadership of pre-exilic Israel. This includes the king, the high priest, the prophets, the elders, and the officials—those responsible for the defilement of the sanctuary and the desecration of the divine name."[5] These rulers had created chaos by not providing the order that would have come about had they acted responsibly. As a result, Yahweh will now provide the missing order.

As in other prophetic works and more so here, Yahweh's new order would provide security for the people. As sovereign protector, he would safeguard his people by his power. In another example of fabulous divine intervention, the story describes the coming invasion by mythical armies led by Prince Gog, but Yahweh's people would need neither walls nor armies because he would destroy all invading armies. The role of the people would simply be to bury the bodies so that the corpses do not defile the land (39:12).

Near the end of the book (chapters 40–48), Ezekiel describes the miraculous construction of a new city and temple, with chapter after chapter detailing the specific geometric plan for the temple, its miraculous construction, and the residence of Yahweh within as promised. The ultimate takeaway from the book of Ezekiel is that their god is the absolute center of their life and would remain permanently with them.

---

5. Milgrom and Block, *Ezekiel's Hope*, 176.

Ezekiel: A Cautionary Tale

An Imposed Upon People—1

As suggested above, the people have little responsibility in this new scenario that the visionary prophet is relating to them. Yahweh seems to no longer trust these vulnerable people to keep the ordinances and commandments given to them. Almost to save them from themselves, in chapter 11, using inspiring imagery, Yahweh graphically declares that he will remove their hearts of stone and create new ones for them. Later, in chapter 18, he specifies how the exiles will become purified and loyal to Yahweh, just as in ancient times the exiles from Egypt were purified in the desert. This curious statement is both a prescription for right living and a fantasized return to a mythical time in the desert when good order reigned between Yahweh and his people.

When the survivors and exiled return to this newly promised country, their god would provide for all the people's needs—the land would be self-sustaining with mysterious waters flowing down from the (imagined) new temple to irrigate the country, producing trees that would bear fruit monthly and have leaves with medicinal powers (47:1-12). These waters would also desalinate the Dead Sea, enabling it to be stocked with fish. In short, Yahweh is all that matters; the only responsibility of the people is to be obedient and to worship him in the right manner. The book ends with the phrase: "God is there" (48:35).

An Imposed Upon People—2

With the emphasis on right behavior and right worship, the role of the priest was writ large. Priests had existed before, but the king was the ruler and cultic leader. Ezekiel accurately prophesied that the monarchy would not be restored and that a particular line of priests who, like Ezekiel, claimed descent from Zadok (the mysterious high priest chosen by David) would lead the country. He justified such specific privilege by referencing an occasion when the descendants of Zadok were supposedly loyal to Yahweh, but other priests were not (44:15). His uncanny prediction proved true: the descendants of David failed to re-occupy the throne and the descendants of Zadok provided the main leadership for the struggling province of Judea for the next 350 years.

Ezekiel's dream was the creation of a theocracy, the rule of a country by a religious leader such as exists in modern-day Iran. Most scholars agree that in the 350 years of the Zadokide priesthood, the country approached but never fully became a theocratic state. Still, the high priesthood was a significant political force in the country. Obedience to the law, the giving of tithes, and performance of the cult were heavy expectations placed upon the people.

Imposition of strict religious observance was justified by Ezekiel's promise of a magnificent future in which Yahweh would give them a self-sustaining kingdom with all their enemies vanquished. Over time, the wonderful promises became a source of anxiety: Why hadn't it happened yet? Religious people could not contain their anxiety. Divisions occurred as different factions claimed to have the answers as to when and how that glorious, or sometimes terrible, future would come about. Their solutions were often brilliant, but their premise that a divine power would miraculously intervene proved false. Ultimately, their tiny kingdom would be overrun by Persians, Greeks, and Romans, just as it had been in the past by Egyptians, Assyrians, and Babylonians.

"Disorder" was the norm. More important, the people themselves were vulnerable to any charismatic leader who promised to confront the presumed disorder and turn back the clock to that mythical past when things were right in the world. Leaders would seek the power to rule, but not always exhibit the courage to confront injustice.

An Imposed Future

Using the familiar, prophetic trope of punishment then redemption, the book of Ezekiel moves from condemnations of Israel and other nations toward predictions of an Eden-like, counterfactual future. In that future time, Yahweh would protect them from all enemies. They could instead turn their attention to the magnificent temple with its accompanying regulations and festivals, which

Ezekiel: A Cautionary Tale

the prophet takes seven chapters to describe. In the final chapters, a greatly enlarged promised land that actually extends north into Syria is described. More importantly, this land is divided into equal shares for each of the twelve tribes, as well as an allotment for the priests. The land itself is thus reordered.

Ezekiel's future predictions would take a strong hold in the Jewish culture. Other futurists would add to or embellish this vision of what was to come: prophets would be taken up to see the heavenly world that was to come down to earth, and others would receive messages from angels. Despite the failure of the future kingdom to appear, the dream of a divine intervention remained alive and even spread to other religions.

Engaging Ezekiel

Ezekiel's description of an ordered paradise is attractive because it touches our deep-seated need for order, which developmentally we all pass through sometime in the preteen years when concepts of rules and fairness are very important. As described by psychologists such as James Fowler, faith in this earlier stage of development is a belief that life works if we all play by the rules. This belief is justified by stories we tell ourselves about how the world works or should work.[6]

Ezekiel's desperate need for order and his insistence upon his god taking care of everything limit our freedom to explore other versions of the transcendent. His story is threatened by other narratives and so requires an authority to enforce the rules and beliefs contained in the one true story; this presumed need easily leads to authoritarianism. A second difficulty occurs when beliefs become as important as behavior, if not more so. Good order requires group thinking and eventually an adherence to a rigid creed. The powerful experience of transcendence that Ezekiel describes so poetically can become misshapen into mere conformity.

Such a conformist and authoritarian community will find it quite difficult to engage with different peoples because the community's psychological boundaries are too rigid. The group believes

6. Fowler, *Stages of Faith*, 135–50.

it needs to protect its special status and so distances itself from others. To listen to other voices or to empathize with other people fosters a more open attitude and supports the critical thinking that threatens a closed community. Although a sixth-century prophet, Ezekiel avoided the insights of other Axial Age visionaries that favored a more universal understanding of the transcendent.

I do not want to live in a theocracy like Iran's, or in countries that are moving in the direction of merging secular and religious power, like Israel and Turkey. Defining the United States as a Christian nation is a similar movement that seeks a religiously-tinged authoritarian government to protect its followers from threats to its nativist ideology. An agnostic can appreciate that such a movement has betrayed the transcendent in the mistaken belief that it is protecting its own survival.

The message I take away from Ezekiel is a cautionary tale that our experience of the transcendent can only be halting and fleetingly described. To draw conclusions from the experience requires the humility to recognize that other people have generally drawn different conclusions from their experiences. By encountering their stories, we can learn about their insights. However, for real dialogue, parties must develop the ground rules for examining different positions and the critical thinking to sort through contradictions and harmful implications.

An agnostic comes to the altar dedicated to this process of critical thinking and eager to experience the transcendent as conveyed in one finite articulation of its power. An agnostic enters into dialogue with this expression of the transcendent knowing that such an encounter can lead to mistaken conclusions, but appreciating that reason can help sort out what is helpful from what is harmful.

Such critical thinking would likely be impossible for Ezekiel, as he appears overwhelmed by his experience and overly invested in his beliefs. His over-investment in the future is an understandable solution to his temporal distress, which is both personal and historical. However, such intense investment makes it unlikely that he would tolerate the current state of affairs with its confusion and ambiguity. Instead, he becomes the apologist for authoritarians

Ezekiel: A Cautionary Tale

who hijack our experiences of transcendence by promising to introduce an idealized future where order finally reigns.

According to historian Gerald Izenberg, the aspiration to transcendence is the rock-bottom component of identity.[7] I can see why Ezekiel, a priest without a temple and an exile without a land, has an identity crisis. His awe-inspiring experience of transcendence offered a way to consolidate his own identity—at the cost of blinding him to the vision of justice and service that were also part of the prophet's mission. His identity was secure, but at what cost to others? He sacrificed to serve a dream that promised paradise but really only justified power.

What happens to someone whose identity is based on a distorted view of the transcendent? Modern believers in any Ezekiel-like story give up something of their own identity in following a cult-like figure who tells or touches upon a deep-seated story that gives meaning to their lives, even if others are treated unfairly. They even ignore or rationalize the self-destructive actions required to keep their allegiance to the authoritarian leader. Their critical thinking appears anesthetized.

Sociologist Arlie Roschchild observed such irrational believing in her five-year study of Tea Party stalwarts and Trump supporters in Louisiana. She concluded that the subjects she studied held a "deep story" about what was happening in America and were impervious to any information that contradicted it. Many were also deeply religious.[8] The failure to address the irrational in religion, even one's private version of it, fostered a belief in a past that never was and a future that never will be. They believed in Ezekiel's story.

Ezekiel worked in Babylon in the first half of the sixth century BCE—that special time Jaspers saw as the heart of the Axial Age. Another major prophet also worked in Judah around the same period of time; his name was Jeremiah. Jeremiah's view of the transcendent took him to an almost opposite position from that of Ezekiel; we will explore his views in the next chapter.

7. Izenberg, *Identity*, 425.
8. Hochschild, *Strangers*, 137–43.

5

The Prophet Jeremiah as Existential Hero?

[Jeremiah's] unflinching and courageous stand expressed one of the essential principles of the Axial Age: people must see things as they really are. They could not function spiritually or practically if they buried their heads in the sand and refused to face the truth, however painful and frightening this might be.

KAREN ARMSTRONG, *THE GREAT TRANSFORMATION*

IN THE FLYLEAF OF her Bible, my grandmother had written: "597 BC Babylonians took the first captives from Judah; 586 BC Babylonians captured Jerusalem." She took few other notes from the scripture class she attended almost a hundred years ago, but those sixth-century BCE dates are critical for understanding the Jewish Scriptures, especially the major Jewish prophets. Their Axial Age insights helped the Jews overcome the destruction, exile, and suppression inflicted upon them by the Babylonians, which began in 597 BCE.

Ezekiel promised a magnificent future, but in the book of Jeremiah, the protagonist embraces the traumatic present. He is

The Prophet Jeremiah as Existential Hero?

tasked to warn the people that they must change their ways and maintain their alliance with the Babylonians. Despite the power of his call and his own charismatic gifts, as well as some connection with prominent scribal families, Jeremiah is portrayed as being ineffective in his own times. However, in the long run, he is seen as successful in fighting for the physical survival of his people.[1]

Despite the historical context in which the story takes place, Jeremiah is better seen as the protagonist of a novel rather than a figure of history. Biblical scholar Robert Carroll compares the attempt to reconstruct the historical Jeremiah with efforts to find the historical Jesus—it's just as impossible.[2] Carroll is not the only one to describe the book as a community project in which various factions of the post-exilic community are both looking for answers and posing questions in the text.

The book of Jeremiah is an epic story of faith, courage, and hope. The book offers its readers an opportunity to relive the trauma and terror of Judah and Jerusalem's destruction so that they can master the experience. Jeremiah becomes more than an exemplar and model for those living in the aftermath of the destruction and the mixed results of reestablishing the nation: he is a therapist helping his patients survive and endure into the future.[3] Unlike the book of Ezekiel, Jeremiah does not offer grand promises of an idyllic future or dreams of a theocratic state. His vision is that of the existentialist hero who faces challenges despite overwhelming odds.

Faith

Jeremiah's act of faith begins with his religious experience. Like other prophets, he is called by Yahweh for a particular task and forewarned that the people may not listen. Faith takes concrete form in the act of believing in a mythical story in which their god chose the Jewish people to be his own. Jeremiah begins his

---

1. Heschel, *Prophets*, 124.
2. Carroll, *Jeremiah*, 63.
3. O'Connor, *Jeremiah*, 45.

catechism with the belief that this god took the Jews from Egypt and formed them as his people in the desert. This Golden Age ended when the people, given the promised land, began to worship other gods. Yahweh is disappointed—he had hoped that by privileging the children of Israel they would call him "my father," but instead they behaved like unfaithful spouses (Jer 3:18–19).[4]

Jeremiah's belief in Yahweh also contains the faith that their god will forgive them for their faithlessness. Although there are some concerns about unjust behavior or people's harsh treatment of the poor, the main thrust of the charge of unfaithfulness is that the people have worshiped other gods. Jeremiah's faith is based on a version of the past in which his ancestors were once monotheists, but over time devolved into polytheists. Modern scholars seriously doubt any historical background to the story of the exodus and confidently assert that the people were originally polytheists, and only much later—likely well after Jeremiah's time—became monotheists.

Like other spiritual pioneers of the sixth century, such as Confucius or the Buddha, Jeremiah is seen struggling to transform his religious experience into something tangible and teachable. He depends on mythical stories to articulate his vision and even to justify and give meaning to the terrible destruction wrought upon Judah, Jerusalem, and its temple in the sixth century BCE. Faith is not simply an ecstatic experience, but one that tries to make sense of the crisis at hand. More than that, Jeremiah's faith becomes a model: he holds onto his vision despite the many challenges and setbacks he faces. Unlike Ezekiel, Jeremiah's faith rests not in a vision of future glory, but in the courageous facing of obstacles and weathering the opposition of his fellow people.

Courage

Yahweh demands a lot from Jeremiah. Chiefly, Jeremiah is to tell the people that they will all be destroyed and is strictly ordered to not even mourn for them. Furthermore, Jeremiah is forbidden to

4. Following biblical references are from the book of Jeremiah.

The Prophet Jeremiah as Existential Hero?

marry or have a family and is thus denied the companionship of a wife and the comfort of children—all so that he can be a model consistent with Yahweh's message. Jeremiah is challenged to go against custom and common sense in a test of his faith. He courageously adopts an absurd position and by his actions becomes a prophetic symbol of what will happen to the people. He actively accepts the loss of possible loved ones to show that they will be forced to accept the loss of real ones in the coming destruction.

However, Jeremiah is not only without family, but also seems almost without friends. Who would want to associate with such a doom and gloom prophet? He does not simply lose friends by his courageous position; he almost loses his life as well. He is thrown into a cistern and left to die because he spoke out in the temple, predicting that the Babylonians would conquer the city. Fortunately, Jeremiah, unlike other prophets killed for such predictions, is rescued and allowed to live.

Hope

If the destruction of Jerusalem was the result of past sins, future generations were promised that they would no longer need to pay off such debts. Jeremiah overturns the past trope that the children would pay for the sins of their parents (27:29-30). Each person would now be accountable for his or her own behavior. Such a change meant that the survivors would have a fresh start. They were encouraged to focus on their own behavior and ignore the backlog of grievances from the past. Yet, there was more.

In a daring piece of writing found nowhere else in the Jewish Scriptures, Yahweh promises to make a new covenant with his people by writing his laws on their hearts and not on stone tablets (31:33). His love would be so powerful that it would make them love and obey him spontaneously. With all people being so empowered, religious elites would become superfluous. "No longer shall they teach one another, or say to each other, 'know the Lord,' for they shall all know me, from the least of them to the greatest" (31:34).

The example of their virtuous lives would make them special to the world. Such a proclamation of prophetic eschatology engendered hope, as well as unrealistic expectations. But at that moment in their history, hope was what mattered. Despite the failure of all exiles to return or all prophetic promises to be fulfilled, the prophet's personal empathic message motivated many of them to chase the dream and work toward its fulfillment. Even his unhappy ending in Egypt would not discolor the brilliant future he painted for them.

Sharing the Trauma

Jeremiah's total investment in his ministry marked him as a fellow sufferer who nevertheless remained faithful. He was assaulted and put in the stocks (20:1–3); accused of treason and threatened with death (26:16–17); beat up and imprisoned (37:15–16); and ultimately even rejected by the king and members of the court, thrown into a cistern, and left to die (38:6). Later, although he favors the group sent into exile, he shares the faith of those left in the land and makes an effort to join in the recovery movement under Gedeliah, the Babylonian-appointed governor. Tragically, that effort fails when Gedeliah is assassinated. In his final humiliation, he is taken by force to Egypt by captors who worship a goddess, "The Queen of Heaven" (44:16–19).

Jeremiah is well aware of the cost of discipleship. In words that still challenge translators, Jeremiah declares that his god has duped him and he has allowed himself to be duped (20:7). A stronger translation would be that Yahweh has raped him and he has allowed himself to be violated.[5] This translation would emphasize how much the prophet identifies with the suffering people of Judah despite all his oracles against them. The price of his ministry is to stay in the city that he knows will be destroyed and mix with people who will soon be raped and violated in the coming destruction.

---

5. Heschel, *Prophets*, 113.

The Prophet Jeremiah as Existential Hero?

Jeremiah's identification with the suffering of his people goes beyond his prophecies and angry outbursts against a demanding god. Scripture scholar David Bosworth points out that in several sections both Jeremiah and Yahweh weep. Seeing the destruction of his beloved people, Jeremiah's tears likely reflect his own helplessness to prevent the wholesale slaughter and destruction of Judah. While Yahweh's weeping is consistent with Mesopotamian and Egyptian mythology in which gods and goddesses weep, weeping emphasizes the profound, empathic attachment of the deity.[6] The level of intense feeling articulated in these sections argues that Yahweh and his prophet closely identify with the people at the time of their deepest physical and psychological suffering.

It's a Story

It is tempting to imagine Jeremiah as the protagonist facing the absurd in an Albert Camus novel. However, such an anachronistic identification fails to capture the stories' therapeutic and community building power. The story of Jeremiah meant something vital to the survivors who would try to maintain their identity in the face of tremendous odds against them. Most significantly, Yahweh had failed to protect them. In the aftermath of Jerusalem's destruction, the provincial capital was moved to Mizpah, overshadowing Jerusalem as an economic and political center. The call to return was not answered by many exiles, who preferred to remain where they had settled in the cities of Mesopotamia and Egypt.

Note that Jeremiah's story is not a record of what really happened. It is an inspirational message that Yahweh has survived and they will also. In fact, their special calling as chosen people has only been burnished by the trauma and violations of the invasion. They are to be lifted up and anointed the moral leaders of the world. Jeremiah is their example, the one who remained faithful despite experiencing challenges and enduring circumstances that might have led even a fervent believer into apostasy.

---

6. Bosworth, "Tears of God," 24–46.

Although the story is at times contradictory, there is another level in which it is coherent. The fictionalized biography of Jeremiah offered a way to make sense of his people's experience of catastrophe and trauma. Jeremiah's struggle was not simply to survive, but to find and articulate meaning in the midst of such difficulties. The book of Jeremiah offered later writers the opportunity to insert ideas into the corpus, thus creating something of a collage as an end product.

Interestingly, commentators on the book of Jeremiah seem to go through their own struggles with the book and often end up at odds with each other. Recently, several commentators have argued for a new level of tolerance based on the premise that scholars have—and always will have—differing interpretations of the book. The present community of Jeremiah scholars isomorphically reflects the tolerance of those post-exilic believers who, at least for a time, built a dedicated community that made room for disparate voices.

Limitations

Modern readers might find little connection to the book of Jeremiah with its hyperbolic promises, faith in a punishing god, and a religious rather than scientific description of history. However, modern organized religion labors under a similar worldview. As long as religion's starting point is a beneficent personal god, explanations for tragedy and catastrophe will depend on keeping this god's hands clean. This is the burden of theodicy, which Jeremiah struggled with because his faith began with a loving god who promised everlasting protection to his people. How can one excuse this god from the trauma caused by the Babylonian invasion?

Likewise, Jeremiah's extravagant claims and Yahweh's punishing rage no longer make sense for many people. The conventional religion of our own time is increasingly found wanting. For example, millennials (those born between 1981 and 1996) evidence the downward slide of allegiance to institutional religion, with only about one quarter regularly attending religious services. Are

The Prophet Jeremiah as Existential Hero?

preachers like Jeremiah still needed to challenge them to look beyond their own security? Or, like the survivors in Judah, do they have access to an inner voice that guides them in moral matters and prompts them to make their own covenant with Yahweh?

Engaging Jeremiah

An agnostic might sympathize with Jeremiah's identification with the victims of war and injustice. An agnostic may also marvel at his motivation to maintain such courageous integrity in the face of so much violence and menace. Some may even interpret the story of Jeremiah as a strategy for dealing with post-traumatic stress, since identification is a first step in the healing process that allows survivors to work through their traumatic experiences and arrive at a more developed and sophisticated identity as valued individuals; survivors are encouraged to move beyond the role of victims and instead take more control over their lives. In this view, Jeremiah was like a therapist whose words and actions not only healed, but also inspired the courage needed to face the future.

It is commonly understood that an agnostic has serious difficulties with doctrines and dogma that seem unbelievable, such as belief in God. For me, agnosticism has to do with not believing in the story. For example, Jeremiah ends with his prediction that Yahweh will unleash an earth-scorching rampage against small neighboring kingdoms like Edom and Moab as well as the superpowers of Egypt and Babylon. His claims that Yahweh will right the scales unbalanced by war reflect his rage against the trauma his people experienced and not a scientific understanding of history.

Just as the story of Ezekiel can be used to support authoritarianism, the story of Jeremiah can support sectarian supremacy: one group claims superiority over another and uses that claim to justify harm and even the destruction of the other.

Religious views have real world consequences, as noted by Alexis de Tocqueville, French political scientist, over two centuries ago: "By the side of every religion is to be found a political opinion, which is connected with it by affinity."[7] We have only to look at the 2016 election to note the affinity between white evangelicals, their literal belief in the biblical stories that involved retaliation against real or imagined enemies, and their support for a candidate who promised to right wrongs and restore justice.

We find our identity in stories and meaning in our lives as we place ourselves in their narrative flow. But, as de Tocqueville pointed out, these narratives can play out in real time in politics. They touch nerves for some people who imagine themselves as victims of injustice. They are vulnerable to self-proclaimed saviors who promise to right the wrongs, just as prophets did centuries before. Challenging the stories means challenging the ingrained belief that a divine being or his appointed will rebalance the scales after real or imagined attacks.

The stories told by the prophets contain an elitism that places some people above others. In Jeremiah's retelling of the story, injustice to Judah trumped injustice to Babylon and Moab. The sense of elitism can justify harm done to others as the simple consequence of righting the scales. The ideal of justice as a universal goal gets warped when it is hypostasized as a god who will enforce justice upon the earth.

The book of Jeremiah asks us to believe in a divine being who intervenes to make matters right—the faithful people will have the last laugh on nonbelievers. Although such a sentiment is alive today in some quarters, it ultimately asks us to believe in the story that Jeremiah did. It professes a mythical past and an apocalyptic future. Belief in a story that pushes solutions to a mythical end time can dull our sensitivity to the myriad examples of injustice such as income inequality and the attendant harm to the poor and marginalized such inequality brings. Belief in an intervening god can undercut our responsibility for change with consequences to our planet should we fail to do so. Is it possible to maintain a position of integrity without believing that some divine power has your back? The message of the Axial Age suggests that we cannot

---

7. De Tocqueville, *Democracy in America*, 300.

The Prophet Jeremiah as Existential Hero?

survive as a species unless we find the means to repair collectively the global damage to justice.

The Axial Age leaders of the sixth century were a gift to all of us; their ideas are part of our evolutionary heritage. Their ideas have been spread and sometimes distorted by followers who try to apply their message in other contexts. In the next chapter, we consider the book of Isaiah in which three different prophets applied their faith in a transcendent Yahweh in three different contexts.

6

Isaiah: Three Prophets in One Book

For centuries, the book of Isaiah was a puzzle. The persons and events referenced in the book covered a span of at least 150 years. How could one person write about such a broad swath of history? The puzzle was solved when biblical scholars showed that the book was easily divided into three sections, each with its own author, but all assuming the name Isaiah. For convenience they are called First, Second, and Third Isaiah.

 First Isaiah lived in the eighth century and is responsible for chapters 1–39. He wrote about a beleaguered Judah that survived war and invasion, but managed to preserve Jerusalem and its temple. His section ends with the Assyrian assault on Jerusalem in 701 BCE. Second Isaiah is an anonymous individual that took the name Isaiah and is responsible for chapters 40–55. This author writes of a devastated Jerusalem with a destroyed temple, but nevertheless prophesies that the people will again rise and be gifted by Yahweh's promised actions. He can be dated to the sixth century because he mentions King Cyrus of Persia, who conquered the Babylonians in 539 BCE and allowed the Jewish exiles to return to their homeland. Third Isaiah, who lived later in that sixth century, composed the last part of the book, chapters 56–66. He described the struggles of the returnees and the factions that arose with no

Isaiah: Three Prophets in One Book

king to lead them. He also references a new temple in Jerusalem, which at the earliest was built about 515 BCE.[1] What unites them all is the common story they told with its hope for a better future.

Part One

First Isaiah: Chapters 1–39

First Isaiah covers a period of at least forty years, given the historical references in this first section, and allows us to see the evolution in Isaiah's thinking. Like Amos, he begins with the assumption of some earlier time when the people of Judah lived obediently with their god. Then they rebelled and became a sinful nation. At first, transcendence is intimately tied in with social justice—for example, rescuing the oppressed, defending the orphan, and pleading for the widow (1:17).[2]

Like Amos, the author is alluding to the income inequality that had emerged in the development of large estates and marginalization of subsistence farmers (5:8). Such a system led to injustice and bribery in the courts (5:23). Since transcendence is embodied in Yahweh, social justice violations would not be tolerated and he would punish the nation for such infractions. Such consequences are believable because First Isaiah is writing at a time when small nations were warring against each other or threatened by the specter of Assyria.

Despite the perilous times of First Isaiah, the author hoped for a time when war would end. "They shall beat their swords into plowshares, and their spears into pruning hooks; nation shall not lift up sword against nation, neither shall they learn war anymore" (2:4). The near future may look bleak, but after the threat of devastation comes the promise of restoration: Yahweh would cleanse the people and restore the kingdom.

The prophet's own spiritual experiences over time led him to develop a more complex sense of divine transcendence that went

1. Leclerc, *Introduction to Prophets*, 162–64.
2. Biblical references are from the book of Isaiah.

beyond social justice. He tells of a vision that emphasizes the impassable gap that exists between his god and humankind. "Holy, holy, holy, is the Lord of hosts: the whole earth is full of his glory" (6:3). Other Axial Age visionaries imagined a more accessible transcendence, i.e., through discipline one could become more in sync with that other world. First Isaiah, however, imagines a fearful other, a transcendence that is awesome and incomprehensible. He cannot speak for Yahweh until an angel cleaned his lips with a burning coal.

And speak he does. In fact, he imagines an ideal king, an intermediary for this unimaginable deity, who will usher in a new golden age. This mighty ruler will bring "endless peace for the throne of David and his kingdom. He will establish and uphold it with justice and with righteousness from this time onward and forevermore" (9:7). This ruler will assure a kingdom in which "the wolf shall live with the lamb, the leopard shall lie down with the kid . . . and the lion shall eat straw" (11:6–7).

While a future leader will bring that heavenly vision to earth, First Isaiah tends to find fault with present rulers. In 734 BCE, Syria and Samaria have teamed up to invade Judah. King Ahaz of Judah consults with the prophet who advises him to trust in Yahweh and not seek help from Assyria. Isaiah offers as a sign the birth of a child who will be named Emmanuel, or "God with us." The prophet predicts that by the time that infant is eating solid food, those two invading kingdoms will be conquered by Assyria. The king does not follow his advice to trust in Yahweh, but instead becomes a vassal of Assyria to protect the kingdom against the invaders. Isaiah responds by predicting that Assyria will have its way with Judah.

A few years later, another crisis occurs. Ahaz has died and his son Hezekiah is now king. Judah again is enticed into joining a coalition to battle against encroaching Assyria, this time led by the Philistines. Isaiah protests against such involvement by walking around naked for three years. His dramatic protest may have worked because Hezekiah, fortunately, does not join the coalition.

Isaiah: Three Prophets in One Book

Judah's lack of involvement pays off. The Assyrians destroy the major Philistine city of Ashdod and thereby end the revolt.

A final crisis occurs in 701 BCE. The Assyrians march on Jerusalem in retaliation for Hezekiah's next rebellion against them. This time the king follows the prophet's advice and the city is miraculously saved. The Scriptures state that an angel of the Lord struck down 185,000 Assyrians and thereby saved the city.

Present-day scholars tell a different story. While it is not clear why the Assyrians lifted the siege of Jerusalem and left the city and temple intact, the invading army destroyed much of Judah. Their king, Sennacherib, boasted that he had conquered all the other fortified cities of the land, brought captives into exile, and exacted tribute from Hezekiah. Archaeologists conclude that Judah was devastated.[3] Isaiah chapters 36–38 suggest that King Sennacherib returned to his Assyrian capital of Nineveh shortly after raising the siege of Jerusalem and there was killed by his sons. In reality, that parricide occurred twenty years later, giving the king many more years to continue his warring ways.

Evolution in the Prophetic Literature

Although First Isaiah is a rough contemporary of Amos, his investment in historical events and specific predictions regarding Assyria and then Babylon (39:5–7) do two things. They reinforce the idea of a true prophet as a predictor of the future and, equally important, maintain that the Davidic monarchy is the vehicle for bringing about transcendent justice upon the earth. However, the real force behind the throne is of course Yahweh—as illustrated by the fate of Ahaz, who refuses to follow the prophet's advice and winds up with his kingdom being exploited as a vassal state of Assyria (2 Chronicles 29:21). Yahweh insures a different outcome for Hezekiah who repents and prays for deliverance: his prayer is answered and his kingdom saved.

---

3. Finkelstein and Silberman, *Bible Unearthed*, 259–64.

Although Isaiah responds to real historical events, his interpretation of them demands that he distort the facts. Several of his prophecies are not fulfilled. Others have more mundane explanations. His prediction that Judah would rebound after Sennacherib's terrible destruction of the country somewhat comes true. The kingdom regains some of its former wealth and status due to a new ruler named Manasseh who trusted more in his political skills than his faith in Yahweh; however, he is subsequently reviled by later Jewish writers as an evil king.[4]

First Isaiah struggles to make concrete how transcendent justice, which is a primary characteristic of Yahweh, can be brought to bear on this earth. Over time, the identity and survival of Judah, the temple, and its Davidic line of rulers all became identified as a test case for divine justice. Guided by Yahweh, the Jewish people are to become the model for a just society. At one point, the prophet predicts that Judah will be an equal to the two superpowers of Egypt and Assyria, even imagining them worshiping Yahweh together (19:18–24).

That hyperbolic prediction never happened, but the underlying sentiment is worth noting. The prophet is counterbalancing Judah's special identity with an obligation to influence other peoples. He articulates in story form what we might call noblesse oblige: Judah's noble status as Yahweh's chosen comes with certain obligations. The people are expected to work for justice by engaging others, as well as by being a model for even the most powerful.

Engaging First Isaiah

What makes First Isaiah difficult to believe is not simply the miraculous stories of deliverance or destruction. The problem is that he has painted himself into a corner. He cannot get heaven onto earth and his efforts to do so, though poetically beautiful, are upturned by critical thinking and scientific data. Even though he at one point sees Yahweh as totally other, he is inspired by his ecstatic

---

4. Finkelstein and Silberman, *Bible Unearthed*, 273.

Isaiah: Three Prophets in One Book

experiences to claim that the kingdom of Judah will accurately reflect the transcendent values of his ineffable god. He even makes a bet that such a transformation will happen and will be recognized by all peoples everywhere.

To an agnostic who values the transcendent, First Isaiah is a warning about what can happen when the religious experience is translated into a concrete action plan. This prophet, like the rest of us, is situated in a particular moment of time and heavily determined by identity characteristics such as political predilection, cultural influences, and other pre-existing conditions. The power of his poetry touches us because it echoes our own religious experiences. We have experienced something wonderful and wish to see it translated to our world. In our enthusiasm, we block out the implausible and the irrational because we believe that following a course of action or a particular leader will bring to earth our experience of the transcendent.

I am an agnostic because I appreciate that the experience of the transcendent is so powerful that it can engulf us and overwhelm our capacity for critical thinking. In what one scholar describes as a "prophetic seizure,"[5] First Isaiah is told to separate himself from the thinking and believing of his fellow Israelites—the otherness of Yahweh has been translated into the otherness of this prophet. Agnosticism that both values the transcendent and one's own capacity to think is a buffer against being seized by an otherworldly experience that claims too much and discounts the opinions of others. The prophet's encounter with Yahweh has led him to isolate himself from his own people. In his isolation, he rewrites history and papers over evidence of his errors. He also sets the stage for Second Isaiah, who must now confront the reality that First Isaiah was wrong. How to reconcile the fate of a broken and leaderless people with the grandiose promises of Yahweh? As one of the most creative and innovative theologians that ever lived, Second Isaiah will bring the transcendent to earth in a way both shocking and comforting.

---

5. Roberts, *First Isaiah*, 136.

Part Two

Second Isaiah: Chapters 40–55

First Isaiah had bet everything on Yahweh's promise to protect Jerusalem, the temple, and the Davidic monarchy. 150 years later, he was proven wrong. Foreign troops broke down the walls of Jerusalem, destroyed the temple, and ended the Davidic monarchy. The natural consequence of such destruction to a small kingdom normally led to the disappearance of its identity and absorption into the larger empire. How did the Jews maintain their identity and persevere as a people?

Much of the credit goes to Second Isaiah, whose creative and stirring theological message instilled hope in a defeated people. His section of the book begins with the claim that he was sent to this broken people to comfort them. "Comfort, comfort my people, says your God. Speak tenderly to Jerusalem, and cry to her that she has served her term, that her penalty is paid, that she has received from the Lord's hands double for all her sins" (40:1–2).

In order to back up this claim that horrific destruction was part of a divine plan and would be followed by great blessings, the prophet built on the insights of Amos and First Isaiah, but then pushed them into a more comprehensive theology. He was promising a better future because Yahweh controlled history and could make anything happen. Additionally, other gods were only human creations. Instead, Yahweh was to be worshipped by all people. In essence, this prophet introduced monotheism: a god became God. In this revision of the prophets' story, the Jews were to play a critical role in bringing to earth God's transcendent justice, but this time the emphasis was on service and not power.

Yahweh the God of History

With earlier prophets, foreign rulers played the role of Yahweh's punisher: when Israel sinned, foreign rulers exacted retribution. Now the story changed. The prophet's ministry takes place after

Isaiah: Three Prophets in One Book

the Persian King Cyrus had defeated the Babylonians who previously had destroyed Jerusalem and exiled many of its people. Shortly after he defeated the Babylonians in 539 BCE, Cyrus established a policy that allowed exiles to return to their homeland and even gave some material support to do so. Expanding on that historical event, the prophet claimed that God had raised up King Cyrus to free the Jews from captivity and help them rebuild their country. He defended this alternative view of reality by claiming that Yahweh made Cyrus his shepherd (44:28) and anointed one (45:1)—titles usually given to the Davidic kings.

The establishment of Cyrus as God's chosen instrument is not simply a one-off divine intervention. Second Isaiah has God claiming that he made his plans from all eternity and no one can prevent their forward movement (43:12). God is in charge of that movement, but has identified the Jews as a special people who are to help in this progressive, linear advance. Their example will inspire other people, thereby contributing to this divinely mandated progress. In creating this novel perspective, Second Isaiah is, according to philosopher Martin Buber, originating the theology of world history.[6]

The One God of All People

With the destruction of Jerusalem, the Jewish religion needed a bigger god. Prior to that time, Jews were like their neighbors—polytheists.[7] Second Isaiah was pulling together and refining theological concepts he both invented and inherited. In addition to being the Lord of history, his God was eternal, the Creator and Redeemer of the world. Second Isaiah tells a new story in which only Yahweh is God. Transcendent justice now had its own avatar who had the power to make things right.

The prophet invoked the almighty power of God to make outrageous promises. The near empty land of Judah would be

---

6. Buber, *Prophetic Faith*, 208.
7. Grabbe, *Judaic Religion*, 215.

crowded with settlers who have returned to the homeland (49:19). The land will be forever be blessed and protected from enemies (54:11–15). The rebirth of Judah will be so marvelous that other nations will turn away from their idols and declare their belief in this one God: "To me every knee shall bow, every tongue shall swear" (45:23). The prophet is promising no less then a new world order in which all people, following the stellar example of the Jews, learn to live together in justice and peace.

With such power, Yahweh can afford to be magnanimous. Unlike Amos and First Isaiah, the prophet describes no day of wrath for other nations. Only Babylon suffers punishment and humiliation because of its destruction of Jerusalem. The real evil becomes idolatry and the prophet makes fun of idols and those who worship them. Yahweh's rage is channeled onto the inanimate objects that compete for his attention. The one and only God commands exclusive worship.

Suffering and Service

By giving Yahweh all the power, Second Isaiah now has to find a role for the people. He does this by introducing a servant figure as the exemplar of faith in Yahweh: "Morning after morning he awakens my ear to hear as disciples do" (50:4). In Second Isaiah's new narrative theology, the servant—either an individual or the nation as a whole—plays a pivotal role in the story. He comforts the downtrodden with divinely inspired messages. He endures suffering at the hand of others, but does not lose faith. Ultimately, his suffering is redemptive: "He was wounded for our transgressions, crushed for our iniquities; upon him was the punishment that made us whole, and by his bruises we are healed" (53:5). This complex idea about a redemptive servant figure is an innovation in religious thinking in the ancient world.[8]

The story of the servant was a counterintuitive solution to a world that valued power and conquest. The story also demanded

8. Blenkinsopp, *Isaiah*, 110.

Isaiah: Three Prophets in One Book

faith from the devastated people of Judah that their particular suffering was not in vain. Recognizing how daring was this claim, the prophet has Yahweh remind his listeners that God's power is not to be questioned. "For my thoughts are not your thoughts, nor are your ways my ways, says the Lord" (55:8). Much like the author of the book of Job, Second Isaiah tells a story in which the protagonist is a humble and unquestioning believer.

By emphasizing the power of belief, Second Isaiah opens up his narrative so that his people may find a role within it. If they have faith in the promises of Almighty Yahweh, they can embed themselves in a story that gives meaning and hope: life is not random nor history meaningless. Instead, history is a stage upon which people play various roles and learn who they are and who they can become. It is the stage in which believers can find the self-revelation of God.[9] According to Karl Jaspers, the working of the transcendent through history is what unifies history and gives it direction. We participate by entering this journey toward a common goal, the unity of mankind.[10]

Second Isaiah's New Understanding of Transcendence

Like other Axial Age writers and thinkers, Second Isaiah saw the transcendent as good. However, he went a step further and personified the transcendent as a loving God. He begins his section of the book by lyrically offering Yahweh's words of comfort to the devastated people. The story goes on to have Yahweh declare how beloved the people are to him: "You are precious in my sight, and honored, and I love you" (43:4). While that love is everlasting, it also appears to be unconditional. Yahweh's actions toward the people are done not for their sake but for his own.

The prophet's theology of history is a dynamic one because God is moving through history and guiding it in a purposeful way.

---

9. Jaspers, *The Way*, 105.
10. Jaspers, *The Way*, 106.

His sense of the transcendent other as loving and powerful introduces the Axial Age theme of humankind's smallness in relationship to that other. Jaspers sees this realization as something new in the evolution of spiritual development. Mankind "experiences the terror of the world and his own powerlessness . . . Face to face with the void he strives for liberation and redemption."[11] For Second Isaiah, that void included the destruction of Jerusalem and its temple, the devastation of the promised land, and the end of the monarchy. He rebounded from that devastation by articulating a vision that matched the highest levels of Axial Age thinking.

In this prophet's vision, redemption was open to everyone. All people had to do was believe in Yahweh, the one God. The prophet was convinced that the predicted miracle of Judah's resurrection would validate that belief and then motivate Jews to assume their role in Yahweh's plan. They are to model what God is like by creating a just society, which will be a faithful witness to the power of God working in the world.

Like his contemporaries in other lands, this prophet realizes the work will be difficult. However, he does not propose the self-discipline of a Buddha or the rational argumentation of a Plato. Instead people are encouraged follow the model of the servant who obeys and suffers, knowing that good will come of his efforts. Consistent with the idea of an all-powerful God, the role of the individual must of necessity be more modest, and even border on passive.

While the Second Isaiah's vision of the transcendent helped them to survive, the prophet's nebulous outline of Jewish identity becomes problematic when the Jewish people try to organize themselves in the utterly new, post-exilic period with no king, temple, or organizational structure to guide them. If anything, he sets the stage for a more conservative, highly devotional identity, which claims to be the only valid response to this total dependence upon Yahweh. Other groups claim different identities, which they believe define the role of true disciples. The search for transcendence is compromised or held hostage by an equally demanding search for identity.

11. Jaspers, *The Origin*, 2.

Engaging Second Isaiah

The breathtaking vision of Second Isaiah is stunning in its breadth of scale and power to inspire. The prophet's vision, like those of his contemporaries in other lands, appears to have burned itself into our DNA. Whether it is a classless society or new world order, heaven or nirvana, we can't seem to escape this dream of the world evolving into a better place, perhaps guided by an unseen hand. That dream still inspires others to, in their own way, bring light to the gentiles: human rights lawyers in China, indigenous people in Latin America, social activists in Russia. Surely our world would be a worse place were we without those who sacrifice to make it better. The contributions of the Axial Age masters have an evolutionary benefit: they help us to survive in times of crisis and against all odds. Behind Second Isaiah's theology is the power such thinking taps into.

How does one hold on to that powerful vision and yet retain critical thinking? For example, Second Isaiah's story can be dismissed because the promises were never met and the idealistic future never arrived. His unmet dream even introduced confusion and conflict as other voices try to understand what went wrong. Religious Jews shifted the blame from Yahweh to their own behavior and tried in various ways to be in tune with this story of a guided history. Prophets, both religious and secular, have continued the story over centuries by making claims of an upcoming future, be it glorious or destructive.

Also, the prophet's unbridled claims block out more nuanced views of human history. Seeing Yahweh as the Lord of history minimizes the random and patterned role of evolution. A more scientifically-based story of the universe is more useful than one in which an almighty power controls everything. Likewise, Second Isaiah's claim about monotheism and dismissal of other views as idolatry undercuts a more tolerant and ecumenical approach that respects the contributions of other Axial Age figures. Such a claim can also inspire an authoritarian belief system that serves to justify violence in its adherents. Finally, his emphasis on an unquestioning submission to Yahweh can fuel a patriarchal culture that uses submission to male authority as an excuse to dominate women and children. Such submission to authority can stifle the freethinking and creative efforts that characterize what it means to be human.

To engage the story of Second Isaiah as an agnostic is to develop an ambivalent position that appreciates his vision without buying into beliefs that pop up in the story like commercials accompanying a TV drama. The challenge is to maintain a scientific inquiry without losing the majesty of his inspiring message. The work is to find that healthy distance from the narrative that still allows one to be in awe of the author's profound spirituality.

No wonder Second Isaiah's powerful narrative brought hope to a scattered and demoralized group of survivors. It even contributed to their continuing existence as a separate people. While it served an immediate purpose, it left unanswered a number of questions about identity, as well as encouraged the spawning of competing voices that argued about what it meant to serve Yahweh. These controversies and disputes can be detected in the final part of the book of Isaiah, the writing known as Third Isaiah, chapters 56–66.

Part Three

Third Isaiah: Chapters 56–66

Second Isaiah was a difficult act to follow. That author's brilliant and creative theology depended upon several unlikely events happening: exiles would stream back to Jerusalem; Yahweh would miraculously restore Judah; other nations would be converted at the sight of this miracle. Because none of those events happened, he left the story at a seeming dead end. This awkward spot was the starting point as the story resumes in Third Isaiah.

For the narrative to continue it needed to make sense of the reality on the ground, which went beyond the failure of Second Isaiah's promises to materialize. Not only had the destruction of the monarchy left a political power vacuum, but also the mixture

Isaiah: Three Prophets in One Book

of survivors and returnees led to great uncertainty about what it meant to be a Jew. If they were to survive as a people, they needed to forge an identity that included establishing boundaries as to who was in and who was out, rituals that celebrated that identity, and a moral code that distinguished them from their neighbors.

Given such momentous challenges, it is no wonder that these chapters "give evidence for the emerging disputes that will dominate the shaping of Judaism."[12] Other scholars put it more dramatically. "Chapters 56–66 revealed a deeply divided community, rife with social injustice and disorder, power politics, despair and hopelessness."[13] Third Isaiah was one voice that cried out for justice while simultaneously defining what meant to be a religious Jew.

Asserting authority and legitimacy against other viewpoints, Third Isaiah connected to the prophetic tradition by beginning with Yahweh's command to maintain justice. However, the author quickly moved to include the identity markers of keeping the Sabbath and holding fast to the covenant. By giving such a religious definition, the author can now logically claim that anyone who follows these prescriptions can be a member of the chosen people: "for my house shall be called a house of prayer for all people" (56:8). Additionally, this theological novelty solves the difficulty of just how the other nations are to be incorporated into God's kingdom on earth: they are to be converted. More responsibility is placed on the people and not on God's overwhelmingly miraculous work.

In this opening gambit, the book also amends the prophecy of Second Isaiah by inserting a middle step between Yahweh and the miraculous recovery of the land. The author is insisting that the people's role is more significant than his prophetic predecessor allowed. Third Isaiah also implicitly introduces a time frame. Work has to be done, conversions have to happen, and disputes settled before Yahweh can introduce the glorious end time.

Third Isaiah also creates antagonists for his part of the story that are not outside conquerors, but members of the community.

---

12. Brueggemann, *Isaiah*, 165.
13. Leclerc, *Prophets*, 361.

He singles out unjust rulers (56:9–12) and idolaters (57:1–13). The book demonizes part of the population—perhaps a majority—as the source of sin and object of Yahweh's wrath. Again, the focus of attention is not the past sins that led to Judah's destruction, but the present sinfulness now excoriated as the major obstacle to recovery.

Following the familiar trope of earlier prophets, Third Isaiah declares that without justice the religious rituals are invalid. Instead, true worship includes care for the marginalized: the oppressed, the hungry, and the homeless (58:1–9). Unless the guilty parties confess their iniquities and seek forgiveness, they will remain outside the fold. Yahweh will again return, but this time as a punisher and not a comforter to his people. Only after this second punishment (the first was the destruction of 586 BCE) comes the time of great blessing and redemption that is the establishment of a heavenly kingdom on earth, which was earlier predicted by Second Isaiah.

The flow of the story is interrupted with a new idea. Yahweh may need help in his campaign to establish justice. Chapter 61 speaks of an anointed one who will bring good news to the oppressed and proclaim liberty to the captives. This mysterious figure appears to be introducing that heavenly kingdom on earth, led by Jews but noticed by the nations. Third Isaiah then reverts back to its obsessive concern with the themes of punishment and restoration. He describes Yahweh's interventions, but at one point is struck by his God's failure to act. In desperation he cries out for the heavens to be ripped open so that Yahweh will come down with fire and earthquake and nations would tremble at the divine presence (64:1–2).

Third Isaiah moves the story along, but ends with unanswered questions and ambiguous predictions. People are divided as to what are the appropriate identity markers for a religious Jew. The future restoration moves further off into the indefinite future. Evildoers are present within the community, although some of them are simply adherents of other viewpoints. Still, the story is powerful enough that religious leaders and writers continue to hope for a final and glorious restoration.

Third Isaiah and Transcendence

These last eleven chapters of the book of Isaiah continued to emphasize the importance of justice, again practically equating Yahweh and justice itself. Justice is actualized in acts of kindness toward the marginalized and is established as a necessary prerequisite for true performance of the religious cult. However, it is not that simple. The effort to bring the transcendent to earth is now thwarted by the need to identify who those just ones are, because true believers are to be rewarded and apostates punished.

Despite the serious conflicts over identity markers, Third Isaiah holds onto the sense of justice inherited from previous prophets, while at the same time emphasizing the importance of reward and punishment. In chapter 58, Yahweh declares that worship is invalid when worshipers do not share the bread with the hungry, shelter the homeless, or cover the naked. In chapter 65 the theme is reprised, but this time it is the righteous who are fed and taken care of, while the rebellious are left hungry and thirsty. The belief in a system of rewards and punishments becomes an integral part of the story.

Engaging Third Isaiah

Third Isaiah is a startling example of the dilemma that occurs when one attempts to operationalize one's experience of the transcendent. How does one try to move from the personal to the political, to identify right and wrong behavior, to motivate others who have not had similar experiences? Efforts to find consensus and practical solutions simply do not live up to the intensity and clarity of the religious experience. It is no wonder that Third Isaiah contains that cry of longing that begins: "O that you would tear open the heavens and come down, so that the mountains would quake at your presence" (64:1).

What we learn from those courageous prophets who tried to bring down the transcendent is that we are on our own. There is no tearing open of the heavens. We are left to our own devices and those of other like-minded individuals to apply our experiences of transcendence to everyday life. The lesson of Third Isaiah is that our efforts will be flawed and in need of attention and revision. Without ongoing oversight and consultation with others, our encounter with something beautiful can turn into a strident and punitive stance toward those with whom we disagree. Third Isaiah played out his anger towards others in fantasy. In the closing verse of chapter 66, he pictures his enemies at the final judgment. "And they shall go out and look at the dead bodies of the people who have rebelled against me; for their worm shall not die, their fire shall not be quenched, and they shall be an abhorrence to all flesh" (66:24).

Third Isaiah wrote under the name of his predecessors because he wanted to keep alive their vision of the transcendence in the midst of a chaotic struggle for power and identity. Miraculously, something of his effort survived. While his poetic prose does not match that of those whose name he took, his effort to bring some direction at a time of deep uncertainty may have had lasting effects. Hope in the prophets' story of transcendence was kept alive for centuries despite the confusion resulting from disparate voices.

Five centuries later, Jesus, the prophet from Nazareth, claimed that his own religious experience authorized his mission to reclaim the destiny of the Jews to be Yahweh's chosen people. He retold the prophets' story and made it relevant to his own times. Later, his followers gradually modified the narrative to fit the changing needs of a changing religious identity. The next chapter outlines the story of that story's evolution into a narrative that sought to preserve the transcendent while providing the followers of Jesus with a coherent identity.

7

The Changing Story of Jesus, the Prophet

And he asked them, "But who do you say that I am?"

MARK 8:29

IF JESUS WERE INTERVIEWED directly about his identity and mission, he may have responded as biblical scholar John Meier described. Meier concluded that Jesus saw himself as a prophet, Elijah-like, and working in Galilee, which had been part of the old Northern Kingdom. Like his predecessor, Jesus was a miracle worker who warned of a future day of reckoning. Additionally, he believed that his words and work would bring that future closer to the present.[1] Like previous prophets, he had a calling or religious experience and a story to tell. His religious experience at the Jordan River echoes that of Ezekiel's at the river Chebar. He proclaimed a coming day of the Lord like other prophets, but with an added urgency: the time was now; repent and believe (Mark 1:15).

Like the prophets before him, Jesus saw his world as terribly out of sync with the heavenly one it was supposed to reflect. Like

1. Meir, *A Marginal Jew*, 1044–55.

them, Jesus was telling a story about how the reconciliation demanded by Yahweh's justice would come about. His prayer called God to live up to the promises and bring down his kingdom so that it would be "on earth as it is in heaven" (Matt 6:10).[2] When he was crucified and no kingdom appeared, his followers initially stayed with the story but over time grew disillusioned. The story had to change.

Constructing a New Narrative

By the year 50 CE, Paul had dramatically changed the story to put Jesus in the center of it all, offering a way for even gentiles to participate as full members without converting to Judaism. Another fifty years later, Luke created a Jesus who was Jewish with gentile leanings. Around the year 150 CE, Justin further tweaked the story and claimed that the Jewish prophets were basically Christians because they predicted the coming of Jesus the Christ.

Paul's Version

The apostle Paul had his own religious experience and believed he was commissioned to retell the story of Jesus in a way that included gentiles. He wrote some twenty years after the death of Jesus and was convinced that the end time that Jesus predicted was coming very soon. Paul modified the Jesus story by emphasizing the resurrection as the drama's turning point. Paul believed that God raised Jesus from the dead and established him as the Messiah, the anointed one, or Christ, who would soon return to establish God's kingdom on earth. As a sign of that future and as a way to help bring it about, Paul believed he was commissioned to incorporate gentiles within God's chosen people—the Jews. Paul was driven to form these hybrid communities because he believed he had little time before the Messiah's second coming. Initially, Paul thought he would live to see that earth-shattering return (see 1 Thess 4:13–16).

2. All Scripture quotes taken from New Revised Standard Version.

The Changing Story of Jesus, the Prophet

Scripture scholar Richard Pervo points out that Paul's description of his own prophetic call, in letters to the Romans (1:1) and the Galatians (1:13–20), was fundamental to his work to bring the message of Jesus to the gentiles and echoed Second Isaiah's own call: "The Lord called me before I was born, while I was in my mother's womb he named me . . . I will give you as a light to the nations" (Isa 49:1–6).[3] Many Jewish prophets included as part of their message the idea that Jews would become an example to the gentiles, who would then imitate the Jews' highly moral life and dedication to Yahweh. Such an inclusion continued an Axial Age theme of universality—the insights were intended to help all people.

Paul's version of this desire for universality was to create hybrid communities of Jews and gentiles that would be united in their faith in Jesus, the Christ. While he still held the Jewish traditions and laws as valuable, if not irreplaceable, for Jews, he held that the saving work of Jesus had made such requirements unnecessary for gentiles. Paul added a final chapter to the traditional Jewish story by claiming that the death and resurrection of Jesus marked the end and resolution of the separation between humans and Yahweh because of their sin. He also claimed that the glorious end of time predicted by the prophets was just around the corner and, like them, he bet on a future that would confirm his present beliefs.

Paul is firmly rooted in the Jewish narrative. In his letter to the Romans, he writes that the gentiles are a graft onto the tree that is Judaism. He appeals to gentiles to respect and even revere the Hebrew traditions even though they are not required to follow them. How, then, does a story so tied up in Jewish identity now expand to include gentiles? And, how can it balance the particular and the universal? Paul's story is an imaginative and creative effort to solve the dilemma. He tries desperately to persuade different groups to move beyond individual identities and assume a common one as followers of Jesus, the Jewish Messiah.

Undergirding his efforts is the cosmic narrative that he shares with the Jewish prophets of the Axial Age. He, too, is concerned by

3. Pervo, "Converting Paul," 129–33.

the gulf that separates Yahweh and his people. Like the prophets Jeremiah and Ezekiel, he imagines that Yahweh must intervene to bridge the gap. Ezekiel wrote of his god's changing hearts of stone into those of flesh. Jeremiah wrote of this god establishing a new covenant that would force people to do the right thing. Paul offers another and different description of how God resolves the problem that came about because of sin. In Paul's story God sends someone, like the suffering servant in Second Isaiah, to appease his own wrath at his people by forgiving them their sin from the time of Adam. More than that, this obedient servant had been raised from the dead and established as the Messiah, the one who would bring God's heavenly kingdom to this earth. It is a Jewish story that seeks to include the gentiles, just as Jesus's fellow prophets of old had tried to do. Those prophets tried to convert other peoples to Judaism; Paul actually brought the gentiles under the umbrella of Judaism as equal partners in the small, dynamic communities he formed.

Paul seems obsessively concerned with the founding and maintaining of these small communities. As a prisoner on his way to Rome, he writes of his hope to travel to Spain to start one there. His communities are small and fragile, at times challenged by other Jewish Christians who do not share Paul's vision of Jews and gentiles together. Yet, this hybrid community becomes Paul's great work, his effort to make the world ready for the Messiah's return.

Luke's Retelling of the Story

Paul tried to universalize the story by creating a hybrid community. Luke, the evangelist, tried to bridge Jew and gentile by creating a hybrid Jesus. Some fifty years after Paul's first letters that tell of his version of the traditional prophetic story, Luke tried his hand. He begins his Gospel not by invoking some call, which legitimates a prophetic mission, but rather claims he is writing the true story of what has happened. He appeals to the Greek values of reason and order as his justification for a story that bolsters beliefs and teachings already received. He likely dedicates his version of the

The Changing Story of Jesus, the Prophet

narrative to a Greek convert who will now be able to appreciate the truth that supports his instruction into the faith (Luke 1:4).

Luke begins his story with Jewish characters and references to the traditional Jewish story. In the early chapters, Luke makes it clear that Jesus is a protagonist in a familiar story that any Jew could recognize. Mary's accepting the role of becoming the mother of Jesus is in the form of a hymn that closely echoes Hanna's song of joy when she is found to be pregnant with Samuel. An elderly, childless couple is promised a newborn like the promise made to Abraham and Sarah. Holy people rejoice that they have seen the Messiah and in their joy sing hymns that fit quite well within the Jewish traditions of psalms and poetry.

Luke's Gospel story concludes much the same way it began—stressing the connection to Judaism. After Jesus gathers his apostles near Bethany, blesses them, and ascends to heaven, they return to Jerusalem with great joy. The Gospel's last line reads, "They were continually in the temple praising God" (Luke 24:53). In this way, Luke begins and ends his narrative with the Jewish religion, suggesting that the Jesus story is firmly placed within the environs of the Jewish story.

However, beginning in the ninth chapter, Luke introduces a different Jesus and veers dramatically from the traditional story he inherited from Mark and Matthew. Up to that point, Luke had been following the outline of Mark's Gospel written several years before and followed by Matthew, who wrote a few years after Mark. Those first two Gospels focused on reaching out to fellow Jews, while any mission to the gentiles remained inchoate. Writing some years later, Luke is aware of the growing prominence of gentiles in the movement and the growing hostility of Jews toward it. Luke needed to explain in narrative form how that happened. He does it by introducing in the middle of the story—between the pro-Jewish beginning and end—a pro-gentile twist to the Jesus story.

Beginning with Luke 9:51, the evangelist breaks off from Mark's Gospel and introduces a unique section that describes a different Jesus and a different understanding of his work. Luke 9:51–10:24 acts as a kind of prologue for his own original material, which extends for some ten chapters before Luke reconnects with Mark's outline in chapter 19. The first thirty or so verses of this singularly Lucan section begins with Jesus determinedly journeying to Jerusalem directly through Samaria rather than bypassing this enemy territory. Religious Jews avoided Samaritans, which is why Mark and Matthew had Jesus bypass Samaria, which likely reflected his deep, Jewish piety. Pious Jewish pilgrims followed that traditional route when they went from Galilee to Jerusalem. (See map below.)

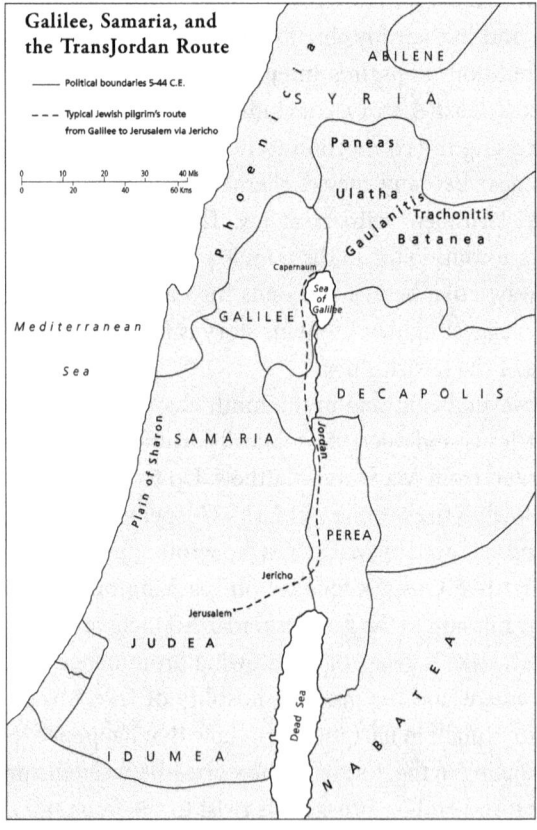

Instead, Luke has Jesus veer off into Samaria, but mentions no Samarian towns, which makes reconstructing that supposed route impossible. In enemy territory, Luke's Jesus stays the course, even

The Changing Story of Jesus, the Prophet

though he is initially rejected by the Samaritans. Along the way he meets would-be disciples and challenges them to agree to an almost unreasonable level of commitment. He then sends out seventy-two of them to the places he will soon visit himself. After they leave, he heatedly condemns Galilean cities where he once preached and worked miracles. When the disciples return, jubilant at their success, he marks their victory with bold claims about their work and his identity. Luke's purpose in retelling the story is hidden in the narrative.

Luke's point of view emerges when his narrative is contrasted with Mark's. The earlier Gospel had Jesus avoid Samaria, stay primarily within a Jewish environment, and die as a "ransom for many" (Mark 10:45). Mark is writing around 70 CE and is focused on Jesus as the Jewish Messiah. Luke's contrasting Gospel makes sense if it were written some years later than originally thought, perhaps in the beginning of the second century CE, at a time when the Christian movement was going through an identity crisis as it evolved from a Jewish sect to a predominantly gentile religion. The evangelist was therefore challenged to present, in story form, a defense of the Christian movement as it faced competition not only from its parent religion, but also from mystery cults and philosophical schools of those times. Luke changes the story for this new audience of gentile believers and critics with the net result that Luke 9:51–10:24 introduces us to a Jesus who is "poles apart" from the protagonist of Mark's Gospel.[4]

In Luke's version, Jesus emerges as a more complicated character. Luke has Jesus set his mind on Jerusalem because he is seeking his destiny in the holy city even if it means his own death. Jesus is a prophet who heroically faces danger not only in Samaria but also in Jerusalem. In the book of Kings, the prophet Elijah fled Samaria and escaped into Judea to hide from his enemies (1 Kgs 19:3). Luke's Jesus does not hide but strides ever forward. When the Samaritans did not welcome Jesus, his disciples called for their destruction (Luke 9:53), but Jesus does not bring down fire upon the Samaritans as Elijah did (2 Kgs 1:9–12).

4. Pervo, *Gospel of Luke*, 197.

Jesus journeys through Samaria because he is better than Elijah. He is a prophet who will not run away from his identity or hide from his enemies. Setting out on a heroic journey, Luke is not describing a savior who comes to take away the sins of the world, but rather a prophet-hero who sets an example for his followers and will accept as disciples only those who demonstrate the same remarkable self-discipline and unquestioning loyalty to the mission as he does. When Elijah's disciple Elisha asked to say goodbye to his parents before following him, Elijah gave his permission—not so with Jesus. Jesus states that anyone pausing for such a farewell is unworthy to be his follower.

Prior to meeting his disciples, Jesus is portrayed as a fiercely independent prophet. However, when he sends them on individual missions, he is suddenly filled with rage and curses the Jewish cities where he ministered. His rage stems from anxiety that his whole career depends on whether his disciples can carry on his life's work. But, with their triumphant return, he is ecstatic and "rejoiced in the Holy Spirit" (Luke 10:21). Jesus's self-awareness changes as he realizes that the success of the disciples validates his own power. To both prospective converts and potential critics, Luke's Jesus points to the success of these disciples not only as proof of God's blessing on his own prophetic movement, but also as proof that Jesus is God's son (10:22). In Luke's Acts of the Apostles, the story of missionary triumphs continues, now powered by the Holy Spirit.

Luke's revised version of the Jesus narrative stresses the universality characteristic of Axial Age visionaries—all are invited to benefit from their insights. However, Luke's major problem was that most Jews refused to believe his story, just as earlier Paul had met with a similar refusal to accept his retelling of the Jesus story. Paul, nonetheless, remained optimistic and opined that Jews would become jealous of the gentiles' faith and would soon convert en masse. To Luke was left the task of explaining how a story that began with Yahweh's chosen Jews had now become one in which these same Jews rejected the movement that claimed to be the fulfillment of their God's promises to them.

The Changing Story of Jesus, the Prophet

Any apologist who began, as Luke did, with Jesus the Jewish prophet would have to explain why God now favored gentiles. Jesus was part of a Jewish tradition that believed that their trustworthy Yahweh would eventually make good on promises made centuries earlier. Luke's gentile audience would question the trustworthiness of this God if those wonderful promises were now transferred willy-nilly to non-Jews. Luke answered the question by declaring that the present generation of Jews did not listen. His Jesus reverses the oracle of the prophet Ezekiel by damning Jewish cities while praising the gentile cities of Tyre and Sidon (Ezek 26:1–28:23; Luke 10:13–15). Jews would be condemned, not because they had become idolaters—the charge leveled against them by Ezekiel and other prophets—but because they did not listen. In Luke 10:13–16 Jesus declares, "Whoever hears you [the disciples] hears me, and whoever rejects you [the disciples] rejects me, and whoever rejects me rejects the one who sent me." Listening to the disciples now becomes the key opportunity for being admitted to or being rejected from God's company. At the end of Luke's Acts of the Apostles, he has Paul say that the Jews did not listen and, so, he would take his message to the gentiles (Acts 28:28).

Like Paul, Luke describes an ambiguous relationship with Jews. However, he goes beyond Paul by presenting a Jesus character that appeals to non-Jews. Luke's Jesus is a hero who stays the course even though he is warned that Herod is plotting to kill him (Luke 13:31–33). Jesus also bests other thinkers at elaborate feasts, scenes that bring to mind the debates of Greek philosophers at similar banquets (Luke 11:37–54). He tells stories, such as the Good Samaritan and the Prodigal Son, that rival those of Greek and Roman storytellers. Luke builds on the earlier Gospels of Mark and Matthew to tell the story of a larger-than-life hero that would be familiar to Greeks and Romans.

Justin's Version of the Story

Justin Martyr is "considered the first true intellectual and professional scholar in the church."[5] He was born around the year 100 CE into a family of Greek extraction in what was once the Northern Kingdom of Samaria. He was determined to become a philosopher and studied with the followers of different schools. In his *Dialogue With Trypho* he describes a conversion experience after meeting an elderly gentleman, presumably a Christian, who convinced him that the philosophies he had studied were inadequate. Instead, he encouraged Justin to study the Jewish prophets who found truth in their encounters with Yahweh. Upon hearing the old man's arguments, Justin wrote that a flame had been kindled in his soul. He was filled with a love of the prophets and for those who were Christians.[6]

Two generations after Paul and one after Luke, Justin developed his version of the Jesus story, this time emphasizing its value as a philosophy and its roots in the ancient Jewish prophets. He began this mission at a critical time in Christianity's development. By the mid-second century, Christians were struggling with an identity crisis that needed to be resolved if they were to survive. Jews by then had rejected Christians as being part of their Jewish religion. Romans saw this now majority-gentile religion as simply a late-arriving superstition, which is how writers such as Pliny, Suetonius, and Tacitus described Christian belief.[7] Supporting their contention was the fact that the Christian movement was split into many separate fiefdoms, often identifying themselves by a particular leader.

Justin faced the same challenge as did the Jewish prophets of the Axial Age: how to present universal truths while at the same time helping a particular people survive in hostile circumstances. He had to take on three opposing forces: the Jews who disowned Christianity, the Romans who saw it as a superstition and, finally,

---

5. Ehrman, *How Jesus Became God,* 330.
6. Justin Martyr, *Dialogue,* chapters VII–VIII.
7. Hayes, *Against Marcion,* 165.

The Changing Story of Jesus, the Prophet

the many versions of Christianity that confused outsiders and perpetuated the notion that it was a superstition. Justin's solution was to latch onto the prophets and redefine them as predicting the coming of Jesus the Christ.

Although previous gospel writers had also argued that Jesus was fulfilling prior prophecies, Justin emphasized that the prophets realized that they were predicting the coming of Jesus the Christ. In other words, the prophets were believers in Jesus—they were Christians. Going beyond Luke, Justin argued that the Jews not only did not listen, but also were now supplanted by a new Israel, the race of Christians.

Justin would argue that this intimate connection with the Jewish prophets meant that Christianity was not some passing superstition, but had deep roots in Jewish history. Justin argued the Christians are the true spiritual Israelites and the descendants of Judah, Jacob, Isaac, and Abraham, led to God through the crucified Christ.[8] The prophets for Justin become not only proof that Jesus is the Messiah, but also the warrant for diminishing the Jewish religion so that Christianity could supersede it. He was also arguing that Christianity should now benefit from the privileges that the Jewish religion had in Roman law and be exempt from offering sacrifice to the idols.

Justin argued that Christianity is the very opposite of superstition. Using the prophets as criterion for predicting the coming of Jesus the Christ, he argued that Christianity was a philosophy, a way of critically thinking about what is true and proper in life. The testimony of the prophets and Christ's teachings, he argued, were the basis for a genuine science and a true source of knowledge.[9] This new emphasis on Christianity as a philosophy tended to minimize the nearness of the second coming and emphasize the task of salvation through right living, which echoed the work of other Axial Age philosophers.

The centerpiece of Justin's thinking was the concept of Logos, a popular term found in Greek philosophy. He saw the same term

8. Justin Martyr, *Dialogue*, chapter XI.
9. Hayes, *Against Marcion*, 70–71.

used in John's Gospel, which begins, "In the beginning was Word (Logos), and the Word was with God, and the Word was God" (John 1:1). Justin maintained that Christ had pre-existed as the Logos, the word of God, and that God created everything through this divine entity. Therefore, this Logos was present in every person by entering into each of them through the process of creation like a seed. Justin could then argue that the best philosophers were touched by Christ and shared in the truth that Jesus announced to the world. In his *Apologia,* and especially in his *Dialogue with Trypho*, Justin made extravagant claims that Christ the Logos so inspired the prophets to predict his own coming as Jesus that they were, in a real sense, Christians.

Justin stripped the prophets from their historical context and placed them in his own philosophical/theological one—and, in the process, denigrated the Jewish religion. Justin argued that the Jews had now been abandoned by God and superseded by Christians.[10] Later Christian writers read his beliefs into the more ambiguous attitudes of Paul and Luke toward the Jews. Justin's version of the story would water the Christian roots of anti-Semitism.

Finally, Justin worked to separate his version of Christianity from other followers of Jesus, which he claimed were inauthentic and inspired by demons. The basis for distinguishing his from these others was his claim that his version represented true belief that could be traced back to the Jewish prophets. He was defining Christianity as a belief system, which could be distinguished from erroneous attempts to construct similar systems. It was the beginning of the movement toward orthodoxy as the defining characteristic of true Christianity, a task that would preoccupy the religion for the next twenty centuries.

Like the prophets he misinterpreted, Justin struggled to balance universal values with the particular identity needs of a threatened people. He offered the Logos as the key to universal truth, which provided a solid identity to anyone who believed in that truth. Error became the ultimate demon and ever to be guarded against. The transcendent Axial Age vision was now contingent upon becoming a true believer.

10. Rokeah, *Justin Martyr,* 134.

The Changing Story of Jesus, the Prophet

Such preoccupation with orthodoxy hid from view the dilemma that Christianity attempted to be both Jewish and not Jewish at the same time. Justin violated the Jewish religion by robbing it of its prophetic core. A simple reading of Justin's works, the *Dialogue* and the *Apologia*, immediately exposes how far-fetched his arguments are. Scripture scholar Robert Miller provides a more detailed approach that invalidates Justin's arguments.[11] However, Justin's efforts can also be seen as an attempt to exorcise the Jewish ghost from the Christian movement by relegating to them the role of villains in a new story made for gentiles. The fruit of all Justin's labors produced a people with a powerful identity. The power of Jesus had been transferred to them and they could now withstand all the assaults that threatened their very existence.

Engaging the Jesus Story

The evangelists and apologists of the first and second centuries were composing a story that would enthrall Western civilization for centuries. In this new narrative, Jesus the Christ was present at the beginning, changed the course of the story in the middle, and would return at the end to usher in a new Golden Age; he became the main character in this revised version of the prophets' story. The Christian storytellers were successful at developing a powerful identity for those who saw themselves as players in the narrative, but at a cost. In addition to falsifying history, its criteria of orthodoxy for membership meant it would demonize differences of belief, a tendency seen even now in religious wars. Also, it would be threatened by the continued existence of the Jewish story it tried to supersede, leading to centuries of anti-Jewish sentiment.

The prophets' story helped the Jewish people survive in the face of conquest and oppression, and the Christian story organized societies, framed cultures, and gave its name to Western civilization—Christendom. The latter story also allowed authoritarian rulers, be they religious or secular, to demonize those who are different and feel justified in their persecution of the Jews. We need

11. Miller, *Helping Jesus*, 227–64.

some kind of "deep story" to give meaning to our lives and motivate us in times of difficulty, even if the story has clearly noxious elements.

"Deep story" is the term Arlie Hochschild gives to the narrative of Tea Party members and Trump supporters that has become a foundation for their view of the world: immigrants, gays and others have cut in front of them, thereby stalling their own journey to the American Dream.[12] Such a story is almost impenetrable because disconfirming evidence usually leads to a reaction that paradoxically entrenches belief in the story's veracity, as noted by social psychologists some sixty years ago in their study of disconfirmed beliefs aptly entitled *When Prophecy Fails*.[13]

However, that same evidence can help an agnostic engage the Christian story without needing to defend it against science's challenge to its truth claims. What if we could imagine a more minimalist Jesus: a prophet-like figure who was flooded with the miraculous vision of the Axial Age? He envisioned people living in justice and harmony led by courageous disciples who would advocate for the poor and seek justice for the downtrodden. Not a pre-existent being, but a charismatic prophet who imagined a better world. This Jesus points to transcendent powers like justice and mercy as ideals to strive for. He offered not a catechism to be memorized, but rather a way of life to be followed. He was offering a version of what Confucius or the Buddha taught about right living. This Jesus can be conjured up in the readings and rituals of a church service where he makes available that Axial Age call for a more just and kindly world.

A minimalist Jesus does not offer a deep story as powerful and all-encompassing as the one that Paul, Luke, and Justin imagined. For an agnostic, however, returning Jesus to his Jewish roots and identity as a prophet works just fine. Retelling the Jesus story in a more historically accurate way offers a better chance of appreciating Christianity's debt to Judaism, while rejecting a theology that still demands conformity of belief as a condition of membership.

12. Hochschild, *Strangers*, 138.
13. Festinger, et al., *When Prophecy Fails*, 3–6.

The Changing Story of Jesus, the Prophet

Jesus is engaged as one proclaiming his version of the Axial Age insights he inherited from the many prophets that preceded him. Like them, he struggled to make the message a universal one. He challenges us to do likewise.

That challenge is to move out of one's comfort zone with its focus on survival (this world or the next) and instead embrace, if only for a moment, this prophet's vision of an alternative reality in which he championed evolutionary friendly behaviors and a fellowship that supported them. It is to lodge oneself in the tension between individual survival and more universal flourishing; between fear and awe; between what is harmful and what is helpful. It is to hold onto something particular in order to glimpse the universal.

A universal story that combines all the contributions of all religions may be impossible, although one that tries to do so is now available. It has yet to develop the Scriptures or rituals of a religion, but it has the beginnings of a narrative that can reintroduce transcendent values, even as our common survival as a people is threatened. This is the story of the universe. The next chapter outlines this story and asks whether it can replace the one begun by the prophets.

8

Science: A New Context for the Prophets' Story?

> In my view, evolution is the story, the meta-narrative of our age. It is not only a scientific explanation for physical reality; it is, rather, the overarching description of reality, the cosmological framework for all contemporary thought.
>
> ILIA DELIO, *THE UNBEARABLE WHOLENESS OF BEING*

THE PROPHETS HAD A story to tell. While they invoked universal values and transcendent themes, their story was immersed in this world. It was concerned about business practices, political treaties, farms, and courtrooms. This real-life focus was sandwiched between a romantic view of the past and an unrealistic hope for the future. Nevertheless, they had a grand story that gave hope and meaning in times of crisis and confusion. Judaism, Christianity, and Islam are all prophetic religions because they tell of a Creator God who enters history, summoning prophets to reaffirm his promises to those who are specially committed to the ideal of justice.[1]

---

1. Haught, *Religion?*, 62–78.

Science: A New Context for the Prophets' Story?

Recent evidence suggests we are abandoning such a grand narrative. Sociologists have described numbers of people leaving traditional religious communities and embarking on individual forms of spirituality.[2] Such a turn inward might well reflect our failure to find a grand narrative. So we tell ourselves stories that are more personal—stories that help us make sense of our lives and the time we have on this earth.

However, a new story is emerging. Scientists were the first to uncover this story that disrupts the familiar ones that have a neat beginning, middle, and end. They tell of a mysterious beginning, "the Big Bang," a present that is fraught with peril, and an uncertain future. This scientific view of our world and the terrible crises that threaten it are the context for a new narrative: the story of the universe. Like the religious story it threatens to replace, this scientifically-based one can overwhelm by its power and mystery.

Reacting to Science

Fear is an understandable response to the power and incomprehensibility of the immeasurable universe and our infinitesimal place in it. The pull of the tide and the tremor of an earthquake can frighten us, as forces beyond our control confront us with the experience of a world too powerful to comprehend. The time frame is overwhelming: fourteen billion years of a life-and-death struggle as elements explode, collide, and annihilate each other. The four-billion-year story of our own planet is also marked by similar violence; the turmoil only lessened somewhat after the planet spent a few billion years cooling down and making itself hospitable to life. After the birth and annihilation of many forms of life, human-like figures appeared over a million years ago, with the actual dates changing as new discoveries are made.

Although our planet seems constant and permanent, it had a rough beginning and will have a violent ending when the sun it depends on collapses in upon itself, likely some hundreds of millions of years in the future. Understandably, we don't much worry about

2. Heelas and Woodhead, *Revolution*, 1–11.

such a distant disaster, but we are increasingly concerned about more immediate and pressing ones. Scientists tell of global climate change, income inequality, and of secondary problems arising from these larger ones; all of this can create fear as a response to our evolving universe. Fear prompts us to close our political and psychological boundaries in a convulsive act of self-protection. Fear prompts us to be concerned with our personal survival and neglect the Axial Age story with its call for justice for all peoples.

Facing such fear does not mean we must grit our teeth and stoically prepare for the worst. Fear and anxiety can be matched by another emotional response to the universe and its mysteries, a response even atheists call spiritual.

The Importance of Awe

Awe is a counterbalance to fear and anxiety. The story of the universe is awe-inspiring to the scientists who study it and the religious writers who ponder over its meaning. They see a movement toward complexity and the emergence of new life forms over billions of years since the Big Bang. Much of this ongoing development comes at a cost, since stars eventually explode and give off more complicated material. It is tempting to imagine that sacrifice for the greater good is part of the pattern. Likewise, mass extinctions can be described as one way in which more adaptive life forms such as mammals crowd out less adaptive ones.[3] Our own species, Homo sapiens, likely crowded out other forms of life we would recognize as human. Evolution continually displays novelty as though bringing forth the new is the key characteristic of the whole process.

Scientist and theologian Alistair McGrath invokes the psychology of awe as a counterpoint to a more fearful view of the wonders of our universe. Reviewing the literature and his own experiences, McGrath sees two components in the response of awe. One is a sense of the vastness of the universe, which is nearly overwhelming in its beauty and incomprehensibility. The second

---

3. Gould, *Evolutionary Theory*, 1296–320.

Science: A New Context for the Prophets' Story?

borrows from psychologist Jean Piaget the concept of accommodation; this latter term captures the change we make to appreciate the vastness of the universe. This change and opening up of ourselves is described as a spiritual or religious experience.[4] One moves from a more self-centered position to one that celebrates the majesty of it all.

Similarly, Jonathan Haidt describes awe as *the* emotion of self-transcendence, in part because it creates an opening for change. A person is less focused on personal concerns and conflicts and open to a more universal perspective. Haidt compares this feeling of awe to psychologist Abraham Maslow's description of peak experience, that sense of wonder that often empowers people to work for positive change.[5]

From Self-Centered to Universe-Centered

The Jewish and Christian traditions have tended to place mankind at the center of this world. In Genesis, God created humans—men and women—and gave them dominion over living things, including plants and fruit-bearing trees. The earth was a paradise subject to the needs and wants of humans. Such a human-centered arrangement worked well for most of human history as mankind gradually invented ways to improve the quality of life. A sudden development called the Industrial Revolution, however, forever changed the course of human history.

The scientific developments, which were steam-powered and coal-driven, were accompanied by a revolution in economics. Capitalism provided the framework for investing in scientific discoveries so as to profit from the sale of new products. While investors took risks investing in new discoveries, the rate of return from such investments exceeded, often dramatically, the normal rate of growth. Such a dynamic led to increased economic disparity between owners and workers. At times, the disparity was partially ameliorated by progressive taxation or regulations that required

4. McGrath, *Reality*, 178–80.
5. Haidt, *Happiness*, 202–6.

owners to consider other factors besides profit. Regulating production by introducing other considerations such as worker safety and consumer protection continues to be an area of significant conflict because a capitalist system is often unable to self-regulate; therefore, the government is often required to step in.

In contrast, self-regulation is the hallmark of the universe. After the Big Bang, chaotic and opposing forces were stabilized into exact relationships that allowed for the progressive movement of matter into more complex forms, including our earth and human life itself. On earth, self-regulation is especially seen in the relationship between the atmosphere and early life forms. To prevent the planet from again being iced over, just enough carbon dioxide was released to provide the right amount of warmth to keep the oceans liquid and life possible.[6] Millions of years ago, when too much oxygen was being released into the atmosphere, organisms developed to consume oxygen while earth's air and water systems helped maintain the right level of that element to foster a flourishing of life forms. This life-sustaining level has been maintained despite the sun's 25 percent increase in temperature over time.[7]

Thomas Friedman argues that since the Industrial Revolution has spread to other parts of the globe, human activity has had an increasing effect on the self-regulatory system of our planet. This human-driven acceleration shows no sign of slowing down, but rather speeds up as more people demand the products and benefits of capitalistic economies. The stress on the earth's ecosystem has threatened the human enterprise: "our Garden of Eden way of Life is now in danger."[8]

On the other hand, scientific progress since the Industrial Revolution has also opened up more opportunities for awe. In addition to the marvelous self-regulatory systems of our planet, we are increasingly aware of our solar system as probes are sent toward its other planets with the promise of unlocking more secrets and explanations of how and why life started on this earth.

6. Sagan, *Cosmos*, 82.
7. Swimme and Tucker, *Journey*, 56.
8. Friedman, *Thank You*, 164.

Science: A New Context for the Prophets' Story?

It has been less than one hundred years since Hubble discovered that there are other galaxies beyond our own. Now, more powerful instruments have been developed to make sense of how these galaxies emerged and whether life forms possibly exist on them. In our efforts to see and appreciate the wonders of life, we briefly touch the transcendent.

Revisiting the Axial Age

The visionaries of the Axial Age offered a way to translate the transcendent into practical applications that gave hope for a better future. Greek philosophers dedicated themselves to the development of reasonable arguments to develop a rational guide for living. The followers of Buddha insisted on a form of self-discipline that would move one towards enlightenment. The anonymous author known as Second Isaiah described heroic suffering as way to bring redemption to others. They all suggested that the solutions to practical problems are within us, especially in our own evolutionary impulse to become more adaptable, more fit, to face the challenges of life.

The Hebrew prophets faced the possible extinction of their identity as a people when powerful nations conquered them. They exhibited the desire and strength to survive despite overwhelming odds. They showed a capacity to look within themselves and find something that gave them the will to survive and the ability to keep their identity. That capacity sprang from a religious experience—a life-changing encounter with a life force they called Yahweh. They described themselves as somewhat passive in the experience, as though this force overwhelmed them and directed them to do things that were extremely difficult, despite their protests that they could not accomplish what was asked of them. Yet their fear ultimately gave way to awe.

Catholic priest and science writer Thomas Berry writes of a similar powerful experience when meditating on the universe: "Awareness of an all-pervading mysterious energy articulated in the infinite variety of natural phenomena seems to be the primordial experience of human consciousness, awakening to an awesome universe filled with mysterious power."[9] Prophet-like, Berry goes on to use this experience of the awesome power in the universe to warn us that we lack a comprehensive story that helps us both to understand the cosmos and to accept our responsibility as a community that influences our planet. That responsibility is now critical because increasingly powerful human technologies threaten the fine-tuned balance evident in the earth's air and water systems. Berry moves from initial awe at the wonder of the universe to a determined commitment to face the man-made problems that threaten our existence in it.

Thomas Berry is not alone in attempting to infuse the data-driven story of the universe with meaning and purpose. Philosopher Alfred North Whitehead believed that the task of philosophy was to integrate religious intuitions and the general ideas of science into a consistent worldview.[10] Reminiscent of Axial Age insights, Whitehead writes that the order and beauty of the world and the creativity and realm of forms with infinite possibilities cannot exist without "the completed ideal harmony, which is God."[11] Whitehead and his followers such as David Ray Griffin suggest that a purely natural philosophy can lead to the divine. Revelation is not necessary.

Others such as minister and self-described scientist-theologian John Polkinghorne are highly influenced by their religious beliefs in their attempts to marry science and theology. For example, Pokinghorne believes that Scripture offers a revealed theology that is separate and perhaps superior to natural theology.[12] Still others, following scientist and theologian Teilhard de Chardin, emphasize the emergence of consciousness from matter and posit a divine presence as part, if not the goal, of evolution. Even an atheist such as astrophysicist Neil deGrasse Tyson feels " alive and spirited and connected" as he contemplates scientific data.[13]

9. Berry, *The Dream*, 24.
10. Griffin, *Reenchantment*, 5.
11. Whitehead, *Religion*, 120.
12. Polkinghorne, *Faith*, 194.
13. Tyson, *Astrophysics*, 198.

Science: A New Context for the Prophets' Story?

Their differing views reveal that the story of the universe does not tell itself. It is told from a particular perspective. The silent universe is a metaphorical inkblot subject to seemingly limitless interpretations.

Becoming Spiritually Scientific

The need to interpret our voiceless universe is important for at least three reasons. Prominent sociologist of religion Robert Bellah argues that any overarching narrative has religious implications because such a story tells us something about who we are and how we came to be.[14] Secondly, ignoring the transcendent dimension to the human experience simply overlooks significant data, such as the Axial Age. It is basically unscientific. Finally, believing and non-believing researchers have shown how positive emotions like forgiveness can lead to a happier and healthier life and that believing in something transcendent can help people recover from trauma. The transcendent is not just there, it helps us to survive and thrive. The problem is how to include this spiritual dimension in the story of the universe.

However, common elements do emerge in the recent attempts at storytelling; they all emphasize the need to make the story our own and apply it to our present circumstances. Like their Axial Age forebears, they describe a world that is good but requires human effort to contribute to its flourishing. Now, even more, that effort is required in order to tackle the man-made crises of our time. In the mythical story told by the prophets, human efficacy was limited because only God could redeem a world so damaged by sin. In the new story told by Berry, the focus is on the damage to our earth that only we can repair. By all accounts, this new narrative is having little effect on repairing that damage. Like the prophets, we face overwhelming forces in our desperate struggle to survive. We can become paralyzed by the immensity of the challenge. If it requires a form of agnosticism to be scientifically spiritual, it requires a kind of faith to be spiritually scientific.

14. Bellah, *Religion*, 46.

Something Like Faith

We are entering the unknown and need something like faith to give direction to our efforts. A century ago, American psychologist William James defined faith as a hypothesis that was both working and alive.[15]

The idea of a working hypothesis comes from science and captures the scientific discipline of tentatively accepting one description of reality, even though the scientist knows it is a working hypothesis that will likely be modified or even overturned in the future. Of course, a working hypothesis means work. It requires engaging the world in a trial and error method—a manner that tries not to hold onto beliefs too tightly, and thus remains open to other perspectives. Hope is not so much investing in a particular story, but in our own capacity to investigate complicated problems and to seek collaborative solutions.

A live hypothesis is one that can grow and flourish through its interaction with real problems. This description of faith emphasizes that it is a struggle, but one that research suggests is critical, especially for emerging adults. Engaging with differing views and wrestling with doubt—rather than discarding religion altogether—helps develop a sense of well-being, as well as contributes to better mental and physical health. It can introduce an inner dialogue that provides a better sense of who one is and what one belongs to.[16] Later in life we have a different struggle; research suggests we tend to stop our spiritual evolution. An active, hypothesis-testing faith depends on our ongoing capacity to think clearly and critically.

David Hunter, following other authors, defines critical thinking as primarily thinking that is aimed at deciding what to believe or what to do.[17] He cautions us that an overreliance on traditional beliefs can short-circuit a more fruitful process of hypothesis testing that furthers our own development: we become more autonomous by examining the evidence carefully before deciding what to

---

15. James, *Will to Believe*, 2–3.
16. Magyar-Russell, et al., "Potential Benefits," 39–55.
17. Hunter, *Critical Thinking*, 2.

Science: A New Context for the Prophets' Story?

believe. Critical thinking is an important cognitive tool for keeping one's faith alive and working. However, a working hypothesis also needs an emotional element.

Openness to the Religious Experience

In attempting to tell the story of the universe, believers and nonbelievers alike have been awestruck by its immensity and mystery. In this way they are similar to the prophets who were awestruck by their encounter with the divine, then pondered about just what this experience meant for them. In the process, the prophets became less fearful and more determined. Finally, they acted despite the overwhelming odds against them and the painful messages they sometimes had to deliver.

However, the openness to the religious experience is being eclipsed in today's scientifically-privileged world. Philosopher Charles Taylor believes that the openness to the transcendent has been minimized in the service of fostering individual rights. He holds that what he calls Christendom with its more narrow focus had to be broken open in order for such rights to be universally accepted and supported. While he supports this breaking open of Christendom, he is concerned that such an individual and imminent focus neglects the more transcendental and universal need for solidarity among all peoples.[18] In a sense, he is echoing what Wilfred Cantwell Smith wrote as the two objectives for humans. The first is to find meaning in modern life, which today's individual focus may help support. However, his second focuses on how to turn world society into world community, which depends on an openness to the transcendent: that sense that there is something beyond one's individual life.[19]

The tension between the particular and the universal will always be with us. The Hebrew prophets also struggled to balance the individual survival of the Jews and the concern that Yahweh be

---

18. Taylor, *Catholic Modernity?*, 17–22.
19. Smith, *Religion*, 183

the God for all people. Religion is one place where this primordial dilemma between individual and community values is celebrated. Although at times parochial and narrow-minded, religion places before us the question, "Who is my neighbor?" It connects us to the prophets' efforts to transcend fear and embrace a religious experience that, at least for the moment, offers a vision of a world community that appreciates the importance of justice and interdependence. Sharing that story, even without faith in God, helps to motivate an agnostic to work for such a community.

Engaging the Story of the Universe

Our efforts to engage a universe so immense and unfinished must of necessity be modest. Our capacity to take in all that data and organize it in story form is just not up to the job. We understandably try to make sense of it by including other narratives, including something of what earlier religious and spiritual visionaries found in their own quests. We can also include the more recent universal call for individual rights even as we hold out for a narrative that calls for the interdependence of all human beings and our joint dependence on our planet. We build on what has existed before, even as we construct our personal, but limited, stories.

To realize that we all have our own stories is to appreciate that truth cannot be our major criterion. A more important question is whether the story is helpful or harmful, to ourselves and to others. It is to focus on the consequences and, more specifically, on our responsibility to treasure that Axial Age insight to work for a more just society. The story of the universe adds another layer of complexity to the challenge laid down by the prophets.

To engage in the story of the universe is to be open to the experience of awe. Believers and non-believers, theologians and scientists urge us to be awed by the mystery and profundity of the universe. The experience of awe can open up for us life-enhancing positive emotions such as compassion, forgiveness, joy, and faith. Psychiatrist George Vaillant studied cohorts of men over decades. In his book *Spiritual Evolution,* he concluded that such positive

Science: A New Context for the Prophets' Story?

emotions contributed not only to the higher functioning of individuals but also contribute to our survival as a species.[20]

On the other hand, to be closed to the experience of awe is to become vulnerable to the experience of fear. While fear and anxiety are part of our makeup, fear-based stories are epidemic, beginning with the policy of some news organizations to emphasize "if it bleeds it leads" headlines. Politicians stoke concerns about economic uncertainty by claiming, often falsely, that certain people are the root cause of all the financial problems and should be punished. Religious leaders say something similar but frame their accusations in religious terms. Such fearmongering chokes off the development of positive emotions and short-circuits critical thinking, both of which are needed to address problems in a more constructive and evolutionary-friendly way.

To engage in the story of the universe is to appreciate and embrace our evolutionary role: the story of evolution contains a moral mandate that we evolve as individuals and contribute to the ongoing evolution of our species. However, humans can only continue to evolve if we take care of our planetary home, the biosphere that supports human life. The story of evolution suggests how we might act our part in this fourteen-billion-year drama.

The vision of the transcendent universe as a self-regulating macro system is an awe-inspiring one that suggests one important takeaway from the science story: we can participate in the story of the universe by imitating it in a small way. Just as our earth regulates itself through multiple systems, we can regulate ourselves to support those systems by limiting some of our activities and enhancing others. Such contributions would help heal the planet and benefit us, as well. These contributions could make the difference between a flourishing future for us and our self-annihilation as a species.

If we need faith to develop a story of the universe, we need agnosticism to protect us from dogmatism. We will never know whether our universe is eternal or one of many universes. We cannot be sure about the fate of our species as our earth continues

---

20. Vaillant, *Spiritual Evolution*, 185–86.

to evolve and tectonic plates crash against each other with severe consequences for the more populated regions of the world. Even the scientific method, with its drive to finding a materialistic explanation for everything, falls short when it comes to understanding transcendent phenomena.

Such phenomena continue to be experienced and then interpreted in a variety of ways. Although many individuals claim their particular insights are superior, an alternative is to tolerate the impossibility of finding such a universal vision that motivates everyone. An agnostic lives with the knowledge that any one version of the transcendent has built-in flaws, but that continued spiritual growth usually needs a structured community that supports that growth.[21] The embracing of a particular tradition is accompanied by doubting the completeness of that tradition's story. The beliefs the story enshrines are always open for questioning and reevaluation. It is this questioning that keeps alive the ongoing search for the transcendent.

---

21. Vaillant, *Spiritual Evolution*, 179.

Conclusion
Searching for the Transcendent

> Moses said to Joshua, "Would that all the people of the Lord were prophets! Would that the Lord might bestow his spirit on them all!"
>
> NUMBERS 11:29

THERE IS GOOD NEWS and bad news about searching for transcendence. The bad news is that our best efforts will always be imperfect. They will reflect our personal and historical contexts despite the intensity of our experience or the beauty of the stories we construct. Just look at the changing story of the prophets. This book is a case study using the prophets to argue for the fallibility of religious story and its corollary that we scrutinize our beliefs for harmful side effects. Wilfred Cantwell Smith made this argument more comprehensively in the 1960s. He looked at several religions and argued that their theological ideas reflect the situations of specific faithful people and their relationship to transcendence at their particular time and place.[1]

In our own times, the growing numbers of the religiously unaffiliated has dramatically underscored the volatile and idiosyncratic expression of religious beliefs and practices. As described by Elizabeth Drescher in her book *Choosing Our Religion*, the "nones" are constructing religious identities that are more cosmopolitan

---

1. Smith, *Religion*, 183.

and relational, as well as include "a number of robust practices that unfold in the context of everyday life."[2] The experience of transcendence increasingly takes more individual forms and expressions.

While we are increasingly on our own when it comes to the meaning and expression of religion and spirituality, there is some good news: we have at least one criterion to evaluate the stories that develop from our experiences of the transcendent. When Moses was praying that all the people (men probably) would become prophets, he was not arguing for individual enlightenment but rather the building up of the community.

Being a prophet is not about predicting the future or preaching about the end times. It is about experiencing the transcendent and communicating to others what you have learned: the individual search for the transcendent has a definite community dimension. Robert Bellah noted that the Jewish prophets were intimately identified with their people. Such identification often deeply distressed the prophets because their people did not change their ways.[3] Scientist Carl Sagan argues that evolution has made us altruistic. He is distressed by the possibility of nuclear war and hopes that our ingrained altruism will eventually conquer our fears and lead us to the policies and politics that demonstrate respect for others.[4] The search for transcendence not only fleshes out our identity as spiritual persons but also requires that we practice community.

For me, that work of translating the sense of sacred into working for a hopeful, common destiny takes place in a particular Christian religion that has been my spiritual home for my entire life. In the small parish I attend I briefly insert myself into the prophets' story by joining in song and response with people from different ethnic groups and of various ages. Some come early to grab a few moments in the quiet church and others come late, often herding children who look with wonder at the stained glass windows. We are all on our separate journeys and with diverse understandings of what we are doing.

---

2. Drescher, *Choosing Our Religion*, 14.
3. Bellah, *Religion*, 317.
4. Sagan, *Cosmos*, 283.

Conclusion

My self-designated role in this community is to try to penetrate the old stories to recover, even briefly, the power of the religious experience. The church's readings from Jewish Scriptures do not prefigure the coming of Jesus, but rather remind me of the evolutionary power that enabled a people to survive and become a model for others on how to do so. The prophets reflected the all-too-human dilemma of developing a particular identity while simultaneously championing universal values such as justice and truth.

The church's readings from Christian Scriptures tell of a Jewish prophet—one who would be quite surprised were he to walk into the church I attend and discover that it was all about him. He approved of being called a prophet but would be mystified by other descriptions.[5] He wrote nothing down in his brief year or so of ministry, but when his followers later told his story, they added layers of wise sayings and miracle stories that enhanced his identity as a prophet and claimed divine backing for his courageous calls for justice. (He was even taken up into heaven like Elijah.) In this process, his followers added a record of their own struggles and retrojected them into the life of one they called their messiah. Going to church means unpacking their additions to the story in order to touch, ever so briefly, the experience of the transcendent and call to conversion that so influenced his life and the lives of his followers.

My task each Sunday is to ask myself why I am here and what is it that I am seeking. I fight against the church's multiple efforts to induce passivity and compliance: the hierarchical arrangement, the required order of service, and the insistence on obedience. I listen to the readings even as I struggle to find their relevance. I realize that there are other sources of wisdom and moral teaching, as well as others who speak out for justice in today's world. However, I have a lifelong relationship with this crucified prophet. I now see him as an avatar of the Axial Age, the personification of justice and love, and the main character in a story of hope that has inspired religious people for centuries.

5. Vermes, *Jesus the Jew*, 224.

Scientifically Spiritual

Albert Einstein warned that a religion without science is blind, but blindness is only the beginning of the problem. To ignore or deny the evidence that religion is about story and not history is to pour sand into the mental processes our species developed to help us adapt and survive. It is to leave the modern world and inhabit a land that refuses to recognize the value of science.

One reason I go to church is because scientists have concluded that it can be helpful. More exactly, they have found that attendance alone is not what benefits an attendee, but actual participation. So I practice community. I check in with the parishioners in the pews near me, join a particular parish group, and generally try to understand and support the parish's work in its own community and beyond. In this community experience, I relearn the lessons of love and forgiveness, joy and compassion, although motivated in part by the knowledge that such emotions are correlated with a long and happy life. Freud's prescription for happiness centered on work and love. Psychologist Jonathan Haidt added a third element. Based on his studies of happy people, he concluded that a connection to something larger than one's self was significant in achieving a happy, fulfilling, and meaningful life.[6]

Even my ongoing investigation of my religion may be a helpful activity. An agnostic neuroscientist argues that practical reason, that way of evaluating a complex culturally-based situation, may be especially helpful in reforming religion.[7] Reform means learning to tolerate ambiguity and to appreciate that our beliefs are provisional. Letting go of certainty, I let go of the old interpretations and dogmatic truth claims to purse a circuitous path through my multi-storied world. Although unsolicited and unrewarded, this investigation is my contribution to the community.

Going to church is also a therapeutic enterprise. In addition to the work of critical thinking, it is the work of constructing and remodeling my own life story while I invest in a more universal

---

6. Haidt, *Happiness*, 238–39.
7. Asma, *Religion*, 208.

one. I often leave with homework: I am self-assigned a task of forgiveness or further research on a particular idea. Often the work is meaningful and occasionally enjoyable, because for a moment I understand something in a new light.

Engaging the religious story as a thinking spiritual searcher also helps to develop a strategy that can inoculate against other noxious stories and behaviors that try to influence us. If we are agnostic about truth claims that cannot be proved, we are more likely to question other claims with little supporting evidence. Knowing that we are terribly vulnerable to stories, we might be better equipped to question those that have a special agenda or likely have harmful side effects. It takes effort to see the false logic and hidden motives of the storyteller.

Going to church is like a workout. You practice community, sign up for projects on justice or classes on mercy and forgiveness. And, once in awhile, you get an uplifting experience, a "high" that brings you close to what the prophets felt. In addition, today's spiritual gym also provides an opportunity to sharpen your critical thinking by challenging a story that claims too much. This workout echoes the "social-spiritual" practices that author and activist Peter Gabel recommends for members of progressive movements, like those seeking environmental justice or extending civil rights to all people. He argues that such practices keep members connected to the spiritual "dawning" that originally inspired the movement and supports its "aspiration to community."[8] Evolutionary movement is both secular and sacred.

Spiritually Scientific

The scientists' story reminds us of our insignificance in the larger scheme of things. After all, we probably owe our existence to a meteor hitting the planet some sixty-six million years ago, destroying the dinosaurs along with many other species of plants and animals. Such massive destruction allowed space for our ancestors,

8. Gabel, *Desire*, 204–6.

the mammals, to take over the niches once occupied by the ruling reptiles. We are not the center of world or the preordained masters of the universe even though sometimes we think we are. Today, we are even more aware of our potential contribution to the future of the planet and realize that, despite the vastness of problems, our actions have consequences. We are caught between the two poles of egocentricity and insignificance. There is no blueprint for specific action but rather an invitation to engage in an evolutionary drama whose ending will escape us. The scientists' story is a new and complicating context for addressing the moral journey of forming one's identity.

Erik Erikson proposed that identities developed by the process of working through various crises over one's lifespan. He implicitly argued that constructing our life stories is a moral and ethical enterprise that requires us to manage one crisis after another and learn to recognize what is a harmful versus a healthy action to take.[9] Professor of Religious Studies William Parsons argues that adequately resolving one's developmental crises "increases a person's capacity for faith, hope and love."[10]

Theologian Bernard Lonergan reminds us of the inherent agnosticism in such a moral journey toward integrity and authenticity. In addition to our more obvious moral failings, we are often challenged to act with insufficient information. We take our best shot at doing the right thing, knowing we may be wrong. Because we act without full knowledge, Lonergan argues that the attempt to live a morally authentic life is really a "fallible, self-correcting process of continuous learning through deliberating, choosing and doing."[11]

The story of the universe's fourteen-billion-year journey magnifies the uncertainty surrounding our own journeys and calls into question the helpfulness of our beliefs. Thomas Huxley coined the term agnosticism in 1869. Some years later, he wrote an essay in which he affirmed that agnosticism was primarily about

9. Erikson, *Identity*, 92–93.
10. Parsons, *Freud And Augustine*, 104.
11. McCarthy, *Authenticity*, 178.

Conclusion

method. He argued, "Do not pretend that conclusions are certain which are not demonstrated or demonstrable."[12] He echoed that ongoing search of Socrates, who likewise stated, "What I do not know, I do not suppose I know."[13] Psychologically, the agnostic is one tolerating doubt and ambiguity as prerequisites not only in the search for wisdom, but also in the construction of one's identity.

However, we are not totally in the dark. I have argued that the story told by the prophets is a transcendent-leaning resource for working out what can give meaning and a moral sense to our lives. Like the prophets, we can fight against the hypnotic attraction to another story that privileges the world's glamor and ruthlessness. We can work for justice, reject idolatry, and look to the transcendent as our guide in times of crisis.

The scientists' story offers a more imminent perspective that likewise challenges us to examine our relationship to the world and our responsibilities toward it. The awe-inspiring story of the universe still needs to be infused with the search for transcendence, even as we become anxious about our own needs for survival. The prophets told stories that described a similar conflict as they applied the insights from their religious experiences to their own precarious situations. Engaging the religious story with its roots in the Axial Age connects us to the many who have boldly and bravely faced that all-too-human dilemma: holding onto the transcendent while trying to survive. In connecting with them, we learn something about ourselves.

12. Huxley, "Agnosticism," 26
13. West, *Apology*, 26

Bibliography

Armstrong, Karen. *Buddha*. London: Phoenix, 2000.
———. *The Great Transformations: The Beginning of Our Religious Traditions*. New York: Alfred A. Knopf, 2006.
Asma, Stephen T. *Why We Need Religion*. New York: Oxford University Press, 2018.
Bellah, Robert N. *Religion in Human Evolution: From the Paleolithic to the Axial Age*. Cambridge, MA: Harvard University Press, 2011.
Berry, Thomas. *The Dream Of the Earth*. Berkeley: Counterpoint, 1988.
Blenkinsopp, Joseph. *Isaiah 40–55*. The Anchor Bible, v. 19A. New York: Doubleday, 2002.
Boccaccini, Gabrielle. *Roots of Rabbinic Judaism*. Grand Rapids: Eerdmans, 2002.
Bosworth, David A. "The Tears of God in the Book of Jeremiah." *Biblica* 94 (2013) 24–46.
Brueggemann, Walter. *Isaiah 40–66*. Louisville: Westminster John Knox, 1998.
Buber, Martin. *The Prophetic Faith*. New York: Macmillan, 1949.
Carroll, Robert P. *Jeremiah*. Philadelphia: Westminster, 1986.
Drescher, Elizabeth. *Choosing Our Religion: The Spiritual Lives of America's Nones*. New York: Oxford University Press, 2016.
Ehrman, Bart D. *How Jesus Became God*. New York: HarperCollins, 2014.
Erikson, Erik H. *Identity, Youth and Crisis*. New York: Norton, 1968.
Festinger, Leon, et al. *When Prophecy Fails*. New York: Harper and Row, 1967.
Finkelstein, I., and Neil Asher Silberman. *The Bible Unearthed*. New York: Free Press, 2001.
Fowler, James W. *Stages of Faith*. New York: HarperCollins, 1981.
Friedman, Thomas. *Thank You For Being Late: An Optimist's Guide to Thriving in the Age of Accelerations*. New York: Farrar, Straus and Giroux, 2016.
Gabel, Peter. *The Desire for Mutual Recognition: Social Movements and the Dissolution of the False Self*. New York: Routledge, 2018.
Gould, Stephen Jay. *The Structure of Evolutionary Theory*. Cambridge: Harvard University Press, 2002.
Grabbe, Lester. *Judaic Religion in the Second Temple Period*. New York: Routledge, 2000.

Bibliography

Griffin, David Ray. *Reenchantment Without Supernaturalism*. Ithaca: Cornell University Press, 2001.
Haidt, Jonathan. *The Happiness Hypothesis*. New York: Basic, 2006.
Hamer, Dean. *The God Gene*. New York: Doubleday, 2004.
Haught, John F. *What Is Religion? An Introduction*. New Jersey: Paulist, 1990.
Hayes, Andrew. *Justin Against Marcion: Defining the Christian Philosophy*. Minneapolis: Fortress, 2017.
Heelas, Paul and Linda Woodhead. *The Spiritual Revolution: Why Religion is Giving Way to Spirituality*. Malden, MA: Blackwell, 2005.
Heschel, Abraham. *The Prophets*. Vol. 2. Peabody, MA: Prince, 1999.
Hochschild, Arlie Russell. *Strangers in Their Own Land: Anger and Mourning on the American Right*. New York: New Press, 2016.
Hunter, David A. *A Practical Guide to Critical Thinking: Deciding What to Do and Believe*. Hoboken: John Wiley & Sons, 2009.
Huxley, Thomas Henry. "Agnosticism." In *Atheism: A Reader*, edited by S.T. Joshi, 25–33. Amherst, NY: Prometheus, 2002.
Izenberg, Gerald. *Identity: The Necessity of a Modern Idea*. Philadelphia: University of Pennsylvania Press, 2016.
James, William. *The Will to Believe and Other Essays in Popular Philosophy*. New York: Longmans Green, 1907.
Jaspers, Karl. *The Origin and Goal of History*. New York: Routledge, 2010.
———. *The Way To Wisdom*. New Haven: Yale University Press, 1974.
Justin Martyr. *Dialogue With Trypho*. Translated by Thomas B. Falls. Washington, DC: Catholic University of America Press, 2003.
Kratz, Reinhard. *The Prophets of Israel*. Translated by Anselm C. Hagedorn and Nathan MacDonald. Winona Lake, IN: Eisenbrauns, 2015.
Leclerc, Thomas L. *Introduction to the Prophets*. New York: Paulist, 2007.
Madsen, Richard. "The Future of Transcendence." In *The Axial Age and Its Consequences,* edited by Robert Bellah and Hans Jonas, 430–36. Cambridge, MA: Harvard University Press, 2012.
Magyar-Russell, Gina, et al. "Potential Benefits and Detriments of Religiousness and Spirituality in Emerging Adults." In *Emerging Adults' Religious and Spirituality*, edited by Caroline McNamara Barry and Mona M. Abo-Zena, 39–55. New York: Oxford University Press, 2014.
McCarthy, Michael H. *Authenticity as Self-Transcendence: The Enduring Insights of Bernard Lonergan*. Notre Dame: University of Notre Dame Press, 2015.
McGrath, Alister. *Enriching Our Vision of Reality*. West Conshohocken, PA: Templeton, 2017.
Mein, Andrew. "The Radical Amos in Savonarola's Florence." In *Aspects of Amos: Exegesis and Interpretation,* edited by Anselm C. Hagedorn and Andrew Mein, 117–40. New York: T. & T. Clark, 2011.
Meir, John P. *A Marginal Jew, Volume Two: Mentor, Message and Miracles*. New York: Doubleday, 1994.
Merton, Thomas. *Mystics and Zen Masters*. New York: Farrar, Straus and Giroux, 1967.

Bibliography

Milgrom, Jacob, and Daniel J. Block. *Ezekiel's Hope*. Eugene, OR: Cascade Books, 2012.
Miller, Robert. *Helping Jesus Fulfill Prophecy*. Eugene, OR: Cascade Books, 2016.
Millgram, Hillel I. *The Elijah Enigma*. Jefferson, NC: McFarland, 2014.
Nagel, Thomas. *Mind and Cosmos*. Oxford: Oxford University Press, 2012.
O'Connor, Kathleen. *Jeremiah: Pain and Promise*. Minneapolis: Fortress, 2011.
Odell, Margaret S. *Ezekiel*. Macon, GA: Smyth & Helwys, 2003.
Parsons, William B. *Freud and Augustine in Dialogue: Psychoanalysis, Mysticism, and the Culture of Modern Spirituality*. Charlottesville: University of Virginia Press, 2013.
Pervo, Richard. "Converting Paul." *Forum* 7 (2004) 127–58.
———. *The Gospel of Luke*. Salem, OR: Polebridge, 2014.
Peterson, Brian Neil. *Ezekiel in Context*. Eugene, OR: Pickwick, 2012.
Polkinghorne, John. *Faith, Science and Understanding*. New Haven: Yale University Press, 2000.
Premnath, D.N. *Eighth Century Prophets: A Social Analysis*. St. Louis: Chalice, 2003.
Roberts, J. J. M. *First Isaiah*. Minneapolis: Fortress, 2015.
Rokeah, David. *Justin Martyr and the Jews*. Boston: Brill, 2001.
Sagan, Carl. *Cosmos*. New York: Ballantine, 1980.
Schreiber, Mordecai. *Hearing the Voice of God: In Search of Prophecy*. New York: Jason Aronson, 2013.
Smith, Wilfred Cantwell. *The Meaning and End of Religion*. New York: MacMillan, 1963.
Stark, Rodney. *Why God?: Explaining Religious Phenomena*. West Conshohocken: Templeton, 2017.
Swimme, Brian Thomas and Mary Evelyn Tucker. *Journey of the Universe*. New Haven: Yale University Press, 2011.
Taylor, Charles. *A Catholic Modernity?* New York: Oxford University Press, 1999.
———. "What Was the Axial Revolution?" In *The Axial Age and Its Consequences*, edited by Robert Bellah and Hans Jonas, 30–46. Cambridge, MA: Harvard University Press, 2012.
Tocqueville, Alexis de. *Democracy in America, Volume One*. New York: Vintage, 1990.
Tyson, Neil deGrasse. *Astrophysics for People in a Hurry*. New York: Norton, 2017.
Vaillant, George E. *Spiritual Evolution: A Scientific Defense of Faith*. New York: Broadway, 2008.
Van Hagen, John. *Rescuing Religion*. Salem, OR: Polebridge, 2012.
Vermes, Geza. *Jesus the Jew*. Philadelphia: Fortress, 1981.
Weber, Elisabeth. "Deconstruction is Justice." *German Law Review* 6 (2005) 179–84.
West, Thomas G. *Plato's Apology of Socrates: An Interpretation With a New Translation*. Ithaca: Cornell University Press, 1979.
Whitehead, Alfred North. *Religion in the Making*. New York: Fordham University Press, 1966.

Index

Agnostic, xi, xiv, xv, xviii, xxi-xxv, 2, 8, 30–1, 49, 57, 64, 82, 91, 94–5, 100–103
Ambiguity, xxiv-xxv, 40, 100, 103
Anxiety, 38, 76, 86, 95,
Amos, xii-xiv, 21, 22–32, 34, 53, 55, 58, 60
Assyria, 9, 12–3, 53–56
Authoritarian, 33, 39–41, 63, 81
Awe, xxii, xxv, 6, 20–1, 41, 64, 83, 86–9, 94–5, 103
Axial Age, xi-xii, xiv, xviii, 1–2, 4–8, 10, 20, 23, 26–7, 30, 32, 40–2, 50–1, 54, 60–3, 71, 76, 78–80, 82–3, 86, 89–91, 94, 99, 103

Buddha, xviii, 1, 3–7, 26, 28, 44, 62, 82, 89

Christian, xiv, xxii, xxv, 8, 19, 40, 75, 78, 80–2, 87, 98–9
Christianity, 78, 80, 84
Church, xvii, xxii-xxiii, 20, 78, 82, 98–9, 100–01
Community, xv-xvi, xix, xxiv, 19, 39–40, 43, 47–8, 65–6, 72, 90, 93–4, 96, 98–101
Confucius, xvii, 1–3, 5–7, 26, 44, 82
Covenant, 35, 45, 49, 65, 72

Critical Thinking, xxii, 31, 40–1, 56–7, 63, 92–3, 95, 100–01
Cyrus, 52, 59

David, 17, 37–8, 54

Elijah, xiii, xiv, 8, 9–21, 23, 69, 75–6, 99
Evolution, xvi, xxii, xxv, 1, 6, 18, 20, 53, 55, 62–3, 68, 84, 86, 90, 92, 94–5, 98
Ezekiel, xiii, 1, 33–44, 49, 72, 77

Faith, xv, 4, 30, 39, 43–6, 48, 51, 56, 60–1, 71, 73, 76, 91–5, 102

God, xiv-xv, xxi-xxiv, 9–10, 16, 18, 20, 22, 26, 28, 31, 33, 35, 37, 50, 54, 58–62, 65–6, 70, 72–3, 76–7, 79–80, 84, 87, 90–1, 94
god, xii, xxiv, 4, 10, 14–20, 24–9, 31, 33–7, 39, 43–4, 46–8, 50, 53–4, 57–9, 72
Golden Age, xxiv, 23–5, 44, 54, 82

Hezekiah, 54–5
Hope, 16, 18, 20, 28–31, 43, 45–6, 53, 58, 61, 64, 66, 68, 72, 84, 89, 92, 99, 102

Index

Identity, xiv, xvii, xxiv, 2, 7, 13, 27, 33, 41, 47, 49–50, 56–57, 62, 64–9, 71, 75–6, 78, 80–2, 89, 98–9, 102–03
Isaiah, xiii-xiv, 1, 26, 51, 52–68, 71–2, 89
Israel, xii-xiii, xxv, 1, 9, 27, 29, 36, 38, 40, 44, 58, 79

Jeremiah, xiii, 1, 41, 42–51, 72
Jerusalem, xiii, 6, 35, 42, 44–5, 47, 52–3, 55, 58–60, 62, 64, 73–5
Jesus, xiv, xxii, xxiv-xxv, 20, 28, 43, 68–83, 99
Jewish, xiv, xviii, xxiv-xxv, 2–3, 5, 6–9, 11, 13, 16, 19–20, 24, 26, 28, 33–4, 39, 42–3, 45, 52, 56, 59, 62, 70–82, 87, 98–9
Jews, 13, 27, 37, 42, 44, 58–60, 62–3, 66, 68, 70–4, 76–9, 81, 93
Journey, xviii-xix, xxii, xxv, 61, 76, 82, 102
Judah, xiii, xxv, 9, 11, 13, 16, 23, 25, 27–8, 35, 41–4, 46–7, 49–50, 52–7, 59–61, 64, 79
Judaism, 65, 70, 71–3, 82, 84
Justice, xiv, xvi, xxi, xxiv, 3, 5, 16, 22–3, 25–31, 33, 41, 50–1, 53–6, 58–60, 65–7, 70, 82, 84, 86, 94, 99, 101, 103
Justin, xiv, 70, 78–82

Love, xxi, 16, 45, 61, 78, 99–100, 102
Luke, 70, 72–5, 77–80, 82

Mark, 69, 73–5, 77
Martin Luther King Jr., 22, 29, 30
Mythical past (see also Golden Age), 17, 38, 50

Narrative, 17, 21, 24–5, 31, 39, 50, 60–1, 64, 70–1, 73, 75–6, 81–5, 91, 94
Nones, xxi, 97

Omride dynasty, 9, 14

Palestine, xii-xiv, xviii, xxv
Paul, 70–2, 76–8, 80, 82
Plato, 3, 5, 7, 26, 62
Prophetic, xviii, 17, 26–7, 29–30, 36, 38, 45–6, 55, 57, 65, 71, 72, 76, 81, 84

Redemption, 2, 26, 38, 62, 66, 89
Redemptive, 60
Religion, xi, xvi, xxi, xxiii, 2, 14–6, 19, 33, 41, 48, 59, 73, 75, 78–81, 83, 91–2, 94, 98, 100
Religious experience, 18, 31, 34, 43–4, 57, 67–70, 87, 89, 93, 99

Samaria, xiii, xxv, 9, 11–3, 15, 18, 21, 23–5, 27–8, 35, 54, 74–6, 78
Science, xi, xxi, 31, 79, 84–5, 89–90, 92, 95, 100,
Scientific, xxii-xxiii, xxv, 1, 31, 48–9, 56, 64, 84–5, 87–8, 90–2, 96, 101
Servant, 60, 62, 72
Socrates, 3, 7, 103
Spiritual, xvii-xix, xxi-xxv, 1–5, 7–8, 19–21, 26, 31, 44, 53, 62, 79, 86–7, 91–2, 94, 96, 98, 100–01
Storytellers, xxiii-xxiv, 77, 81
Syria, 39, 54

Temple, 36–8, 41, 44–5, 52–3, 55–6, 58, 62, 73

Index

Transcendence, xiv-xv, xxi, 7, 21,
   39, 41, 43, 53-4, 61-2, 67-8,
   97-8, 103
Transcendent, xiv-xviii, xxii-xxv, 5,
   16-7, 20, 23, 25-6, 31, 33-4
   39-41, 51, 55-9, 61-2, 67-8,
   80, 82-4, 87, 89, 91, 93,
   95-9, 103
Universal, xiv, xxv, 2-3, 7, 10, 19,
   27-8, 40, 50, 71, 78, 80,
   83-4, 87, 93-4, 96, 99

Universe, xvi, xxii, 63, 83, 85-91,
   93-5, 102-03
Violence, xiv, 10, 14-6, 18-21, 25,
   33, 35, 49, 63, 85
Yahweh, xii, xiv, xxiii-xxiv, 6, 9-10,
   13-9, 23-9, 33, 35-8, 43-7,
   49, 51, 53-67, 71-2, 77-8,
   89, 93